Ways with Food

Ways with Food

By Harriet Healy

Drawings by Marta Cone

DOUBLEDAY & COMPANY, INC.
GARDEN CITY, NEW YORK
1982

Permission gratefully acknowledged for the use of "Simca's In-dividual Cheese Soufflés with Tarragon Cream Sauce" taken from *SIMCA'S CUISINE* by Simone Beck in corroboration with Patricia Simon copyright © 1972 by Simone Beck and Patricia Simon. Reprinted by permission of Alfred A. Knopf, Inc.

Library of Congress Cataloging in Publication Data

Healy, Harriet, 1899–
Ways with food.

Includes index.
1. Cookery.   I. Title.
TX715.H3964   641.5
AACR2
ISBN 0-385-17846-8
Library of Congress Catalog Card Number 81–43568

TO MY SON PAT

who encouraged me to write this book, and his cooking family: Judith, his wife; my grandchildren Patrick, Jr., a chef in France; Alison, a chef in Boston; and Timmie, age eight years, who can wait on tables and eat!

Acknowledgments

I am grateful for the wonderful friendship of Archie and Ora Archambeau and for their help in making Au Bon Goût a success. Without Ora this book would never have been completed.

With thanks to the following: Charlotte Farrar and Jacqueline Cardelli, friends over the years, for their advice and help; Ruth Ingram, who is never too busy to write a recipe or letter; and Bessie Robinson, for her daily assistance in every way.

Working with Jean Anne Vincent, senior editor; Doreen DeFlorio, assistant editor; Diana Klemin, art director; and Marta Cone, artist, on this book was such a happy experience.

Last but not least, I am grateful for the inspiration of four perfect summers in France, made possible by my friends Julia Child and Simone Beck.

Contents

NOTE: *Whenever the name of a recipe is followed by an asterisk (*) in the text, the recipe is included elsewhere in the book. Consult the Index for page numbers.*

When I decided to write this book, it was not my intention to write a complete cookbook, as this has been so well done by my friends Julia Child, Simone Beck, James Beard, and many others. Nor is it written for the novice in the kitchen, as there are many excellent books for the beginner. Rather, I have written for people who know and like good food and have been brought up in America, enjoying foods from all countries of the world.

In 1950 I started a small cooking school in Palm Beach called Au Bon Goût, with only three pupils the first year, and ending in 1965, when I always had a full class. These pupils came from all parts of the country and were eager to learn about cooking, taking lessons because they could not get experienced help or because of their desire to cook for themselves. To this day I find that cooking enthusiasts are always looking for fresh ideas, new recipes, and simpler ways of using all our wonderful American products. So here are some suggestions, showing Harriet Healy's Ways with Food, and many ways of changing basic recipes. The variations, with different ways of serving food attractively, help your menu planning. The choice of wine is left up to your individual taste and selection.

The use of the Cuisinart (or other food processor) and blender is found throughout the book, with some shortcuts and timesaving ideas. There are many inexpensive recipes—and some that are not! So this book is a mixture for people who know and enjoy good food and entertaining.

Bon Appétit,
Harriet Healy

Ways with Food

Suggestions

Suggestions, Recipes, and Tips

BREAD AND CRACKER SUGGESTIONS

I find few people want to eat much bread, so here are some that I serve which are quick, easy, and with not too many calories.

PEPPERIDGE FARM SOUR FRENCH ROLLS

These are very good. Simply heat and serve.

PITA BREAD

Split in half and toast until lightly browned. Butter well (I use clarified butter) and return to oven to crisp. Serve plain or sprinkle with sesame seeds or Parmesan cheese.

THOMAS' ENGLISH MUFFINS
THREE WAYS

1. Toast and butter.

2. Toast and, instead of butter, try spreading with mayonnaise mixed with various herbs.

3. When partially frozen, slice off one end so muffin will fit in Cuisinart feed tube and, with slicer, slice paper-thin. Crisp in 325° F. oven, then pour clarified butter over the small slices. Replace in oven, stirring until butter is well absorbed and slices are crisp. Store in tins. (Clarified butter does not become rancid as quickly as regular butter, so I always use it if I am going to prepare ahead of time.) Sprinkle with seasoned salt to your taste for cocktails. They are also good with soup.

MELBA TOAST

Toast slightly a regular-size piece of bread of your choice (I prefer Thomas' protein). Remove from toaster, place folded paper napkin over top, since toast is still hot (*important*), and slice through horizontally with a serrated knife. Place the thin slices on cookie sheet in 325° F. oven until crisp. These can also be buttered with clarified butter and reheated.

Pepperidge Farm's thin-sliced bread can also be used.

Refrigerate in tightly covered container.

FLOUR TORTILLAS

Break in half after heating in 300° F. oven until crisp and lightly browned. Salt or add other seasonings to your taste and butter if desired.

SAUTÉED TOAST

Use Pepperidge Farm regular or thin-sliced bread, according to your taste. It must be stale, so leave out for about 3 hours or, if in a hurry, place in a 250° F. oven for about 5 minutes, or until dry but still not toasted. Sauté on both sides in clarified butter.

CORNMEAL CRISPS

1 cup yellow cornmeal
½ cup sifted all-purpose flour
½ teaspoon salt
¼ teaspoon baking soda

2 tablespoons melted butter
⅓ cup milk
Sesame seeds (optional)

Preheat oven to 350° F. Sift together cornmeal, flour, salt, and soda, then mix in butter and milk. On lightly floured board, knead dough 6 or 8 times or until it holds together. Break off nickel-sized pieces and sprinkle with sesame seeds (optional). Roll into very thin 4-inch rounds, leaving edges ragged. Bake on ungreased cookie sheet 15 minutes, or until golden. Just before serving, brush with more melted butter and sprinkle with salt. These may be kept for a week in a closed container.

MAKES ABOUT 24

CREAM POPOVERS

4 eggs
2 tablespoons all-purpose
  flour

1 cup heavy cream, whipped
¼ teaspoon salt

Beat eggs and gradually stir in flour, then fold in whipped cream and salt. Butter cast-iron popover pan or Pyrex cups and heat them in oven. Fill almost full with batter and bake in preheated 400° F. oven for 20 minutes, then increase to 425° F. for 15 or 20 minutes.

These popovers are unusual and different. They are like slightly puffed Yorkshire puddings (never high and crisp). In addition to serving them as popovers, you may serve them with maple syrup for breakfast, or as a luncheon dessert with maple syrup and a dab of whipped cream on top.

MAKES 8

SOUFFLÉ CRACKERS

1 (3½-ounce) box Uneeda
  crackers

Ice water
Butter

Preheat oven to 500° F. Soak crackers in ice water for 8 minutes. Drain. Place soggy crackers on ungreased cookie sheet and dot with butter. Place in oven. Bake 10 minutes, then turn oven down to 375° F. and continue baking for 45 minutes, until brown. These can be made several days ahead and kept crisp in well-sealed food container.

An amusing telegram was received from an Au Bon Goût cooking class pupil saying, "I placed cubes of ice on crackers and ran them under the broiler. They were soggy!"

CLARIFIED BUTTER

This is an easy way to clarify butter and always have it on hand.

Clarified butter is most important for sautéing all kinds of foods, as it may be heated to a higher temperature without burning.

Take 4 pounds salted butter and heat it in a double boiler. When melted, pour butter into a larger bowl than it needs. When cool, cover with plastic wrap or foil and refrigerate. The next day remove from refrigerator, run knife around the edge of the molded butter, lift it up, and throw away the milky liquid in the bottom of the bowl. With a knife, scrape the top and bottom of the hard butter so that all the white residue is taken off, then rinse under cold water. Cut butter into 3 or 4 sections and place in containers with covers (mark with freezer tape on the outside). Put 1 or 2 containers in the refrigerator and freeze the rest. It keeps well in the refrigerator and indefinitely in the freezer.

CROUTONS

Using Pepperidge Farm white bread that you have allowed to dry, cut off crusts and cut into tiny squares. Pour clarified butter over and mix well so all sides are coated with butter. Bake in 375° F. oven on a cookie sheet, stirring several times until all croutons are brown and crisp. Freeze in a plastic bag so they will always be available.

1 large egg white = 1 ounce or 2 tablespoons
1 egg yolk = ½ ounce or 1 tablespoon

Freeze egg whites in ice cube tray, 2 whites to a section. When frozen, place in plastic bag and return to freezer. (This can also be done with fish or chicken stock so that you always have stock on hand.)

Beating egg whites: Egg whites should never be beaten in a crockery bowl. They tend to become watery. First choice: a copper or other metal bowl. Second choice: glass. Third choice: hard plastic.

To hard-boil eggs: Place eggs, at room temperature, in water to cover and bring to a boil, then turn down to boil gently for 10 minutes. Take pan at *once* to sink, pour off boiling water, and shake pan madly to crack all the eggs. Quickly pour cold water into pan, letting water run while you peel the eggs. This method is from Graham Kerr and it never fails!

If you are going to make stuffed eggs, stir eggs while they are cooking to keep yolk in center.
Never put stuffed eggs in refrigerator, as it toughens them.

OEUFS MOLLET

Place room-temperature eggs in boiling water for 4½ minutes, then plunge into a bowl of ice water. Peel and serve cold. To serve hot, place peeled egg in slotted spoon in hot water just to reheat.

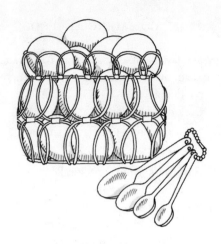

FREEZING SOUFFLÉS

Double or triple any of your recipes for cheese, chocolate, or any other kind of soufflé. Make your soufflé recipe and put the unbaked mixture in soufflé dish right up to the top (frozen soufflés do not rise so high in baking). Freeze overnight, then run a knife around the inside of the dish and place it in warm water for a few seconds. Put a piece of foil, large enough to wrap the soufflé, on the counter and turn the soufflé out of the dish. Wrap, mark, and return to freezer. Keep for 3 weeks at most. When you wish to bake, undo the foil and put the soufflé back in the same-size soufflé dish in which you molded it. Bake in 375° F. oven, with a pan of water underneath, for about 1 hour.

You can prepare the entire soufflé, unfrozen, 1 or 2 hours ahead, cover it until baking with an inverted large bowl or pan, and then bake it. This is my friend Julia Child's idea, and it is so helpful to make it before your guests arrive.

A soufflé prepared and baked immediately is the best; second-best is the one prepared an hour before baking, and third is the frozen one.

We have very good frozen commercial foods in the United States, and there are times when we all use them gratefully. Here is a list of particularly good ones, with different ways of using them. Two packages will serve 4.

1. Stouffer's spinach soufflé
2. Stouffer's asparagus soufflé
3. Stouffer's cheese soufflé
4. Stouffer's corn soufflé
5. Stouffer's French bread pizzas
6. Stouffer's creamed chipped beef
7. Stouffer's chicken Tetrazzini
8. Stouffer's Welsh rarebit
9. Pepperidge Farm puff pastry

SPINACH AND CHEESE SOUFFLÉ

Here is a good combination. Defrost soufflés and place the spinach one in the bottom of your own soufflé dish. Fold into the cheese soufflé 1 beaten egg white, 1 tablespoon Worcestershire sauce, and ¼ teaspoon dry mustard. Place this on top of the spinach soufflé. Bake in preheated 375° F. oven for about 10 to 15 minutes. Serve with a well-seasoned Mornay sauce or Welsh rarebit, to which you have added mustard and Worcestershire sauce to taste and a little cream to thin it.

ASPARAGUS SOUFFLÉ

Defrost 2 soufflés and place in your own baking dish, preferably a shallow oval one. When baked as directed, place 3-inch tips of cooked fresh asparagus around the sides and serve with Hollandaise Sauce*.

CORN SOUFFLÉ

Defrost and place in your own casserole as many as you need and bake in preheated 375° F. oven 10 to 15 minutes, then decorate by covering entire top with fried slices of green or red tomatoes.

PIZZA HORS D'OEUVRE

Prepare frozen French bread pizzas as directed on package. When done, cut into thin strips, then cut each strip in half.

CREAMED CHIPPED BEEF

Remove from cooking pouch and place in pan. To each package add a full tablespoon Worcestershire sauce, plus ¼ cup thin cream. You may vary flavorings, as in my Dried Beef in Cream* recipe.

CHICKEN TETRAZZINI

To the defrosted Tetrazzini add wine or dry vermouth, or curry powder to taste. Bake in preheated 375° F. oven for 10 to 15 minutes. The addition of turkey or sweetbreads plus a little cream with more cheese on top is also an improvement. The original sauce is a little too thick for my taste.

WELSH RAREBIT

For a hurry-up Sunday night dish, defrost the rarebit and place in pan, thin with a little cream, and season with Worcestershire sauce and dry mustard to taste. When hot, top slices of fried tomato with the rarebit and place 3 rolled, sautéed pieces of bacon on top (place toothpicks in bacon rolls when sautéing). A sautéed piece of toast can be put under the tomatoes if you wish. This, served with a green salad, is very good.

PUFF PASTRY

This Pepperidge Farm product is very good as is; however, if you wish to give it more of a butter flavor, defrost, spread soft butter over one or both pieces, fold them over, and roll. Place in refrigerator for about ½ hour, then roll to desired thickness. Cut into crescents, or into any shape you wish, with a cookie cutter and bake as directed on package.

GLACE DE VIANDE

(*Cooked Brown Beef Stock*)

Always have glace de viande on hand, as it is important to the preparation of many dishes. The recipe for preparing this can be found in most good cookbooks; however, as a time-saver, the prepared product is obtainable from *Maison Glass, 52 East 58th Street, New York, New York 10022.*

ICED TEA

2 cups sugar (or less to taste)	5 or 6 sprigs of mint
3 quarts boiling water	Juice of 5 lemons
½ cup black tea	

Boil the sugar in ½ cup water for 5 minutes. Pour the 3 quarts boiling water on the tea, cover, and let stand for 3 minutes. Strain and add the sugar syrup and mint. Cool. Remove the mint and add the lemon juice. (*Lemon juice must not be added until the tea is cool.*) This keeps well in refrigerator. To serve, pour over ice cubes.

SERVES ABOUT 14

ICED TEA VARIATIONS

In Italy, when peaches are very ripe, they are mashed through a fine sieve (or use a Cuisinart) and added to iced tea. This is delicious served at teatime, adding just enough purée so you can taste both peaches and tea. Decorate with sprigs of fresh mint.

ITEMS TO FREEZE AND HAVE ON HAND
FOR THE AVERAGE HOUSEHOLD

Egg whites
Chicken stock
Fish court bouillon (stock)
Purée of Peas*
Clarified Butter*
Beurre manié (see page 134)
A rich Béchamel Sauce*
Bordelaise Sauce*
Sara Lee pound cake
Frozen soufflés (see pages 10 and 11)

Whipped Cream*
Croutons*
Beef stew (minus vegetables)
Lamb stew (minus vegetables)
A few chickens, chops, and steaks
Frozen soups—your own
Frozen crêpes

The first three items can be frozen in plastic ice cube trays, placed in plastic bags, and stored in the freezer for future use.

This is a list of items to have on hand, which is helpful when renting a house or returning home after a long trip. Copies of this list make a thoughtful present.

Canned Food
Campbell's beef consommé and beef broth
A good chicken stock or broth
Sardines, tuna fish, salmon, and ham
Evaporated milk
Tomatoes and tomato paste

Sauces and Condiments
Ketchup, Worcestershire, and chili sauce
Maple and Karo syrup
Salad oil and mayonnaise
Vinegar, all kinds
Major Grey's chutney
Grey Poupon Dijon mustard

Staples
Hot and cold cereals
Sugar—granulated, brown, and confectioners'
Flour
Salt
Peppercorns, white and black
Coffee—regular and decaffeinated
Tea
Dry mustard
Bay leaf
Fines herbes or favorite dried herbs
Cloves and cinnamon or favorite spices
Baking soda and powder
Knox unflavored gelatin

Rice
Fresh vegetables, including potatoes, onions, carrots, and celery
Fruits, including lemons, and juices
Bread
Bacon and eggs
Milk, cream, and butter
Powdered milk
Paper towels, napkins, toilet paper, and facial tissues
Foil, wax paper, freezer wrap and tape
Ziploc plastic storage bags
Plastic garbage bags
Light bulbs
Woolite
Hand and liquid soap
Scouring powder
Liquid bleach
Ammonia

Emergency Items
First-aid kit
Sterno with stove
Candles and matches
Bottle, wine, and manual can openers
Paring knife
Flashlight and batteries
Fire extinguisher
Masking tape (to tape windows)
Drinking water
Wines and liquor of your choice
Battery-operated radio—and batteries

    FOR HURRICANES: Canned foods
                          Dried milk

Remember to fill bathtubs with water (in case your water is turned off during the storm) and turn the refrigerator and freezer to the highest setting to best retain the cold temperatures if your electricity is cut off.

MENU SUGGESTIONS

I often serve a first course for either luncheon or dinner in pot de crème cups, or you can use individual ramekins. Serve all with a teaspoon.

1. Creamed mushrooms flavored with dry vermouth and topped with tiny buttered crisp croutons or Pepperidge Farm herb-seasoned stuffing.

2. This is a quick and unusual pot de crème for hot weather. Serves 4 or 5.

1½ (10½-ounce) cans
Campbell's beef consommé
¼ teaspoon curry powder

4 ounces, or half a large
package, of cream
cheese

Mix the ⅔ can consommé, curry powder, and cheese in blender or Cuisinart, pour into cups or ramekins, and refrigerate overnight. The next day, pour ½ inch of the remaining consommé on top of each cup. Refrigerate. It will jell and be ready for luncheon or dinner!

3. Cold chicken custard made with a strong homemade chicken stock, with or without curry powder, and topped with crumbled bacon.

MUSHROOMS

To clean, place water in a bowl and add about 1 tablespoon flour. Immerse the mushrooms, stir with your hands, and remove from the water. You will see all the dirt in the bottom of the bowl.

DECORATED MUSHROOM

A quick way to do a decorated mushroom for many dishes is as follows: take a firm, raw mushroom (*essential that it be ice-cold*) and peel in swirls with a lemon zester. Broil, steam, or sauté and place on top of anything that you wish to decorate. (A steamed mushroom shrinks less.)

PARSLEY EN PLUCHES

This means the parsley is picked off leaf by leaf and used for decoration on a sauce.

QUICK COURT BOUILLON

When you do not have a court bouillon for fish, use clam juice.

TART FILLINGS

Suggestions for individual tart fillings for a first course, using Cuisinart Piecrust*:

1. Fresh crab meat mixed with a little mayonnaise. Arrange a slice of smoked salmon, cut to fit top of tart, over the filling and garnish with a spray of parsley and capers.

2. Creamed oysters seasoned with a little Worcestershire sauce and sprinkled with crumbled crisp bacon.

3. Rich custard (no sugar) mixed with chunks of lobster or crab meat and flavored with sherry.

4. Cheese custard sprinkled with crumbled crisp bacon.

5. Creamed sweetbreads with crumbled crisp bacon on top.

6. Lobster Newburg, curried shrimps, or creamed mushrooms.

PIECRUST SUGGESTIONS

1. Try making deep-dish chicken pie and deep-dish fruit pies by taking a paper pattern of the top of the baking dish. Make pastry separately the size of the pattern, bake, and place on top at the last minute. This ensures that the crust is always crisp at serving time and also enables you to judge how much sauce has cooked away, so you can add more.

2. For meat pies, season pastry with rosemary, tarragon, or fines herbes.

TOMATO JUICE OR BLOODY MARY HINT

Serve with a rim of fresh parsley around glass or cup by brushing the rim with egg white and pressing it into finely chopped parsley.

Adding bottled horseradish, to taste, makes a very good bloody mary.

TOMATO PETALS

These are used in decorating many recipes for salads, vegetables, and aspic.

Cut peeled tomato in quarters and scrape all the inside away, leaving only the outer meat. These petals will drape nicely over an aspic mold, bunches of beans, asparagus, etc.

TOMATOES PREPARED FOR PEELING

In Sweden I learned a trick from Emmie Berg—a way to keep tomatoes ready for instant use. Blanch them, but do not peel, then return them to the refrigerator until ready to peel and serve.

WHIPPED CREAM

If you have any leftover whipped cream, place on cookie sheet in small mounds, freeze uncovered, and, when frozen, remove and place in plastic freezer bag. To use, remove from freezer and, when at room temperature, beat and stir with a wire whip.

Sauces

Sauces
and Dressings

If you are afraid of making Hollandaise* or Béarnaise* sauce, try these simplified, easy interpretations of classic sauces. Both may be made 2 or 3 hours before serving and reheated at the last moment. To do this, do not cook the sauces completely; keep them on the thin side, and when they are reheated, they will reach the correct consistency. This way, the sauce is always hot for serving.

I learned the simple recipe for Hollandaise Sauce* from my dear friend Emmie Berg when we were at the Cordon Bleu in Paris. She had worked in the kitchen of the Royal Family of Sweden, and this is how they made it and the Béarnaise Sauce*.

Emmie Berg has written several cookbooks and also gave lessons at Au Bon Goût.

HOLLANDAISE SAUCE

4 egg yolks   Salt and pepper to taste
3 tablespoons hot water   1 stick (¼ pound) butter
2 tablespoons lemon juice

First: In a saucepan, beat the egg yolks with a wire whip until thick and pale in color. Add the hot water, lemon juice, salt, and pepper and beat again.

Second: In another pan, heat the butter over medium heat and, when bubbling, pour it slowly into the egg mixture, removed from the heat. Then return to the stove and cook over medium heat, stirring constantly, until sauce is the right consistency, raising pan from heat several times when steam appears, to prevent curdling.

If it curdles, add 2 tablespoons cold light cream or a piece of ice and beat like mad, off the stove. If ice is added, remove it the moment the sauce is smooth.

SERVES 4

(*Variations for Hollandaise*)

1. Stir in 2 scant tablespoons Escoffier sauce Robert and 2 tablespoons chopped parsley. Good on filet mignon or steak.

2. Stir in 2 tablespoons each tomato paste and chopped parsley.

3. Stir in 1 tablespoon melted glace de viande.

4. Make Hollandaise with Spice Islands tarragon vinegar instead of lemon juice. Before serving, stir in 2 tablespoons chopped parsley. Wonderful with fish. Capers may also be added.

5. Mousseline Sauce—half Hollandaise and half whipped cream.

6. Mousseline Sauce for fish—use heated clam juice instead of water.

7. Stir in 2 scant tablespoons green peppercorns.

8. Stir in horseradish sauce to taste.

9. Add chopped mushrooms, or sliced if preferred.

BÉARNAISE SAUCE

Cook 6 finely chopped shallots and 3 crushed peppercorns in ½ cup wine vinegar and ½ cup tarragon vinegar (white wine may be used instead of wine vinegar) until liquid is reduced by half. Proceed as for Hollandaise Sauce*, but add 2 tablespoons of the reduced vinegar, in place of lemon juice, after putting sauce back on stove to thicken. Watch carefully and beat constantly, as in Hollandaise. When sauce is the right consistency, stir in 2 tablespoons chopped fresh tarragon or 1 teaspoon dry tarragon. Good on eggs Benedict or cold roast beef.

SERVES 4

Sauce Charron

For a variation, top Béarnaise Sauce* with chopped fresh peeled and seeded tomatoes. Delicious on sautéed veal, vealburgers, Pounded Lamb Many Ways*, or Hamburger*.

BÉCHAMEL SAUCE

(Basic White Sauce)

2 tablespoons butter
3 tablespoons all-purpose
flour

2 cups milk, half-and-half, or
cream
Salt and pepper to taste

In a saucepan, melt butter, add flour, and, with wire whip, stir over medium heat until smooth. Add milk, half-and-half, or cream, and continue stirring until sauce becomes thick and smooth. Cook for at least 5 minutes, beating all the while. Add salt and pepper.

You can add many ingredients to this sauce, such as chicken stock, onion juice, grated cheese, white wine, dry vermouth, fish stock, tomato purée, egg yolks, or whatever you wish.

If you wish to make sauce ahead of time, cover with wax paper to prevent crust from forming. To use, remove paper and scrape clean with spatula.

NOTE: I do not heat my milk or cream before adding to the roux (butter-flour mixture). It takes longer to thicken, but you save washing another pan!

BORDELAISE SAUCE

1 cup dry red wine
3 tablespoons minced shallots
1 clove garlic, chopped
6 peppercorns
2 tablespoons butter
2 tablespoons all-purpose
flour

1 (10½-ounce) can
Campbell's beef consommé
1 teaspoon tomato paste
3 tablespoons glace de viande
(optional)

First: Simmer the red wine, shallots, garlic, and peppercorns until wine is reduced by half. Strain.

Second: In a saucepan, melt the butter, stir in the flour, and cook until mixture is cheesy in appearance. Gradually stir in the consommé and tomato paste and cook, stirring, until sauce is thickened. Stir in the strained wine and glace de viande and continue to stir over medium heat until well blended.

NOTE: This sauce may be frozen and reheated. Taste before serving, since wine varies and salt may be needed.

This recipe can also be prepared by using 1 (10¼-ounce) can of Franco-American beef gravy instead of the beef consommé and flour.

CUISINART MAYONNAISE

1 whole egg	White pepper
2 egg yolks	1 tablespoon fresh lemon
¼ teaspoon dry mustard	juice or wine vinegar
½ teaspoon salt	2 cups olive oil

Place the whole egg, yolks, mustard, salt, and pepper in Cuisinart and blend with knife blade, then add the tablespoon lemon juice or vinegar. With machine running, start adding oil in a fine stream, increasing as it begins to thicken. Taste for seasonings, adding more salt, pepper, lemon juice, or vinegar as needed.

This mayonnaise can be changed by adding blanched watercress leaves, spinach, parsley, basil, tarragon, or chives. Drain greens and squeeze in 3 thicknesses of paper towels, then add to mayonnaise before you have quite finished blending. Good on fish.

You may also add sour cream or a beaten egg white to lighten the texture.

MY FRENCH DRESSING

(To have on hand in a jar)

1 or 2 cloves peeled garlic
⅓ cup vinegar
1½ teaspoons salt
1 cup olive oil

½ teaspoon Grey Poupon
Dijon mustard
2 shakes Worcestershire sauce

Cut slit halfway through garlic and place in jar with vinegar (I use several kinds mixed, such as tarragon, garlic, or red wine). Add salt and allow to remain overnight (this makes the garlic mellow). In the morning, add olive oil of your choice. For diet reasons, I use half olive oil and half Wesson oil for everyday use. When I have guests, I use the best olive oil (Italian) or walnut oil and make the dressing the same way. Add ½ teaspoon Grey Poupon Dijon mustard and two good shakes of Worcestershire sauce.

MAKES 1⅓ CUPS

The above two French dressings are for your everyday use, but when making a tossed salad, it is always best to make just enough dressing for the occasion right in the salad bowl after rubbing it with garlic (optional). Add seasonings of your choice and then toss the salad.

PESTO SAUCE

(With thanks to the Italians)

1 cup olive oil or half olive
    and half vegetable oil
2 cups fresh basil leaves
½ cup parsley leaves
3 or 4 cloves garlic (some are
    stronger than others)

1 teaspoon salt
½ cup pine nuts (pignolias)
¼ cup grated Parmesan
    cheese

Place all in Cuisinart and process with the knife blade for 3 to 4 minutes until a fine purée. If you are going to freeze it, add the cheese only when ready to serve.

SERVES 6

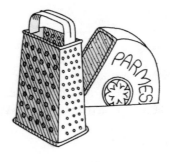

Here are six ways the Pesto can be used:

1. With Tomato Sorbet* instead of curry mayonnaise.

2. In an omelet.

3. In potato salad.

4. Over hot julienne zucchini.

5. On sliced tomatoes.

6. Tossed with all kinds of pasta, which is my favorite!

DIET TARTAR SAUCE

Here is a mixture to pinch-hit for tartar sauce. Combine 1 teaspoon finely chopped sweet pickle, ¼ teaspoon Spice Islands Beau Monde seasoning, 2 teaspoons each minced capers and finely chopped parsley, 1 teaspoon tarragon vinegar, and ¼ cup yogurt.

SAUCE VINAIGRETTE

1½ tablespoons Dijon
   mustard
2 tablespoons red wine
   vinegar

1 teaspoon salt
3 twists black pepper
6 tablespoons olive or peanut
   oil

In a small bowl, mix the mustard and vinegar, using a wire whisk. Add the salt and pepper. Add the oil slowly and continue mixing to form an emulsion. Keep in closed jar and refrigerate if necessary.

In my opinion, a clove of garlic sliced halfway through improves this dressing. Simply add to the jar before refrigerating.

Aspics
and
Hors d'Oeuvre

Aspics
and Hors d'Oeuvre

HAVE YOU EVER THOUGHT OF . . . ?

1. Stalks of endive spread with cream cheese flavored with Worcestershire sauce; or, for dieters, cottage cheese and Worcestershire sauce.

2. Sautéing toast, then spreading it with finely ground round steak seasoned with onion and Worcestershire sauce, running it under a broiler for a second, and serving with a pickle slice on top.

3. Hollowing out a square of Pepperidge Farm toasting white bread, or a thick slice cut from unsliced bread, sautéing in butter, and filling with a good grated Cheddar cheese topped with crumbled bacon.

4. The same sautéed square with chopped creamed oysters and bacon on top.

5. The same sautéed square with creamed mushrooms chopped fine and flavored with dry vermouth.

6. Cutting raw zucchini with a fluted knife and serving them with sauce of sour cream and dill.

7. A slice of apple with a slice of cheese (New York State sharp Cheddar, Crema Danica, Roquefort, Camembert, or smoked) on top.

8. Making a paste in the blender of smoked salmon, cream cheese, sour cream, capers, and lemon juice. Spread on pumpernickel.

9. Smoked dried beef brushed with butter and heated in oven until it crinkles.

10. Breadsticks rolled in thin sliced bacon and broiled.

11. Shrimps or crab meat mixed with seasoned mayonnaise, on an artichoke bottom, an attractive first course for luncheon or dinner.

12. Crisp Potato Skins for Hors d'Oeuvre*. Also good spread with Dried Beef in Cream* or sour cream, grated onion, and caviar.

13. Pizza Hors d'Oeuvre*.

ARTICHOKE FLOWER

Cook 1 large artichoke (see Artichokes [Basic Recipe]*), adding 2 tablespoons olive oil and 1 clove garlic to water. Drain and cool. Remove leaves and arrange them, spreading out around small center of artichoke. Place ½ cup cooked medium shrimp in mayonnaise, or chopped hard-boiled egg, with or without curry powder, on each leaf. (You will need ¼ pound shrimp and 2 hard-boiled eggs.) Or, to be more economical, mix chopped shrimp and celery in mayonnaise.

In place of the shrimp, use any cooked fish, crab meat, lobster, or smoked oysters, mixed with a mayonnaise base, with or without chopped celery, and adding curry powder, chili sauce, mustard, or whatever you choose to the mixture.

SERVES 8

BASIC ASPIC

(A quick version)

2 envelopes Knox unflavored
  gelatin
1 (10½-ounce) can
  Campbell's beef consommé
1 (10½-ounce) can
  Campbell's beef broth

1 soup can water
1 bouquet garni (parsley,
  fines herbes, and 3 crushed
  peppercorns, tied in
  cheesecloth)
⅓ cup dry French vermouth

Soften the gelatin in 3 tablespoons consommé and set aside. Heat the remaining consommé and the beef broth and water to boiling point with the bouquet garni and simmer for 20 minutes. Discard bouquet garni and stir in the softened gelatin. Bring to a boil again, add the vermouth, and cool to lukewarm.

This makes a soft but molded aspic. If weather is hot and you cannot control temperature, or you prefer a firm aspic, increase gelatin to 2½ envelopes.

MAKES 5 CUPS

PIXIE MOLDS

(*Bite-size*)

Rinse Pixie molds, which may be found in most kitchen shops,* in cold water and place 1 teaspoon aspic in each mold. Refrigerate until set.

Below are different fillings that you place on the set aspic, then fill to the top with more aspic and refrigerate again.

Before serving, unmold by running knife around edge and remove onto a cookie sheet with a teaspoon. Refrigerate. When ready to serve, place each on a 1-inch round of sautéed toast and top with a dot of mayonnaise and sprig of parsley.

BASIC ASPIC* MAKES 3 DOZEN MOLDS

Suggestions for fillings:

1. Cooked crab meat, lobster, or shrimp, shredded.

2. Mashed sardines with a squeeze of lemon juice.

3. Finely chopped mushrooms, sautéed in a little butter.

4. Pâté de foie gras.

5. Any soft cheese.

6. Everglades Egg Curry Ring*, using ½ recipe.

7. Chili Sauce Aspic*.

8. Cream cheese, grated onion, and caviar.

9. Cream cheese with curry powder.

10. Dried beef in Horseradish Aspic*.

* Any tiny containers may be substituted for the Pixie molds.

CELERY RINGS

Wash and clean green pascal celery. Cut 12 stalks the same length. Stuff with one 8-ounce package cream cheese flavored with onion juice and Worcestershire sauce to taste. Interlock 3 stalks of stuffed celery. Place in wax paper and roll tightly, twisting ends. Refrigerate for 3 hours (*not* in freezer). Remove paper and cut in ½-inch slices. Serve on ice-cold plate, with a thin round of bread underneath each ring if you wish.

MAKES ABOUT 48

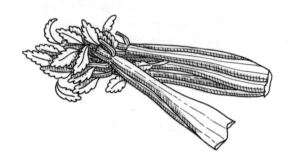

CHILI SAUCE ASPIC

(*Bite-size*)

Simmer for 20 minutes 1 (12-ounce) bottle chili sauce, ½ minced green pepper, 1 chopped onion, a few drops of Tabasco, pinch of salt, and 1 cup water. Mash thoroughly through a sieve. Soften 2 teaspoons unflavored gelatin in ¼ cup water. Add to hot sauce and stir.

Finely chopped water chestnuts or minced lobster or crab meat may be added to this aspic. Mold as suggested in the recipe for Pixie Molds*.

MAKES ABOUT 2 DOZEN

CHEESE CRUNCH

1 cup sharp yellow Cheddar
  cheese
1 stick (¼ pound) butter
1 teaspoon Dijon mustard

1 cup all-purpose flour
Cayenne pepper to taste
2 (⅝-ounce) packages or
  1½ cups Rice Krispies

Cut the cheese into small pieces (⅓ pound = 1 cup), put into bowl of Cuisinart, and process with knife blade. Add the butter (cut into pieces and at room temperature), mustard, flour, and cayenne. Process until smooth and well mixed.

Remove blade and stir in Rice Krispies by hand.

Form into small balls, place on cookie sheet, and bake in preheated 350° F. oven for about 20 minutes.

These can be frozen, either before or after baking.

MAKES 2 TO 3 DOZEN

SHE-CRAB ASPIC

(*With thanks to Hector Ubertalli*)

1 (8-ounce) package cream
  cheese
1 (10½-ounce) can
  Campbell's beef consommé
1 (16-ounce) can she-crab
  soup

1 envelope Knox unflavored
  gelatin, softened in ¼ cup
  of the consommé
Sherry, dry vermouth, or
  curry powder to taste

Soften the cream cheese and beat in the consommé, reserving ¼ cup. Then add the she-crab soup and gelatin, softened in the remaining ¼ cup of consommé. Season to taste with sherry, vermouth, or curry powder. Pour into a fish mold, of at least 3-cup capacity, and place in the refrigerator until set.

SERVES 6

CLAM ASPIC

2 envelopes Knox unflavored
  gelatin
2 pint bottles clam juice
  (Doxsee, if possible)
½ teaspoon Worcestershire
  sauce
Juice of ½ lemon
1 hard-boiled egg

Watercress
Chopped parsley
Red pimiento
Black caviar (optional)
Raw celery root, thinly sliced
Mayonnaise
Curry powder (optional)

Soak gelatin in a small amount of clam juice. Heat to simmering the rest of the clam juice with the Worcestershire sauce and lemon juice. Stir in the gelatin and let the liquid boil up just once. Rinse a ring mold with cold water. Fill it one-quarter full with aspic and put it in the refrigerator for about ½ hour to set. Decorate with slices of hard-boiled egg, watercress leaves, chopped parsley, bits of red pimiento, and black caviar (optional). Drip about 2 tablespoons of the aspic over the decorations and chill until aspic is set. Then fill mold with aspic and chill again. When ready to serve, dip the mold for a moment, almost to the rim, in hot water and turn out onto a chilled platter. Fill center with thinly sliced raw celery root mixed with mayonnaise. Add curry powder to mayonnaise, if you wish.

Decorate the platter with tomatoes and watercress. If you choose to chop some canned clams (about 1 small can) and stir them into the aspic, this is also very, very good.

SERVES 6

EVERGLADES EGG CURRY RING

(For buffet, hors d'oeuvre Pixie molds, or first course for luncheon)

2½ cups Campbell's chicken
   stock or 2 (10¾-ounce)
   cans*
1 tablespoon curry powder
2½ envelopes Knox
   unflavored gelatin

1¼ cups Hellmann's
   mayonnaise*
3 hard-boiled eggs
Pinch of salt and pepper to
   taste

Bring the chicken stock to a boil and add the 1 tablespoon curry powder to the gelatin, which is dissolved in ¼ cup water. Refrigerate until it starts to thicken. Blend in the mayonnaise and fold in the very finely chopped hard-boiled eggs. (Eggs can be done in food processor, using knife, with off-and-on method.) Add salt and pepper to taste. Pour into wet 6½-inch ring mold and refrigerate until set.

Remove from mold by placing hot wet towel over mold and running knife around sides and middle of mold. Decorate top of egg aspic with 1-inch Tomato Petals* placed at intervals on top. Dip watercress or lettuce in French dressing to place around and in center, if desired.

As a first course for luncheon, mold in small Pyrex dishes and serve on rounds of sautéed toast.

SERVES 6

* Homemade stock and mayonnaise are not necessary when using curry.

HORSERADISH ASPIC

1 envelope Knox unflavored
  gelatin
Juice of 1 lemon
1 teaspoon Worcestershire
  sauce
1 tablespoon onion juice

2 tablespoons mayonnaise
1 pint sour cream
1 pinch dry mustard
3 tablespoons bottled
  horseradish

Soak gelatin in 2 tablespoons cold water until soft. Add ½ cup boiling water and stir until the gelatin is dissolved. Add the strained lemon juice, Worcestershire sauce, and onion juice.

In another bowl, combine the mayonnaise with the sour cream. Pour the liquid mixture into this, adding the dry mustard and horseradish. Mix thoroughly, pour onto a platter, and refrigerate until jelled. When serving, place thinly sliced cold roast beef on top.

Another way of serving is to make small molds or cut rounds of the aspic and place them, each on a slice of tomato, around the sliced meat.

For a delicious variation, add some sautéed paper-thin dried beef, in shreds, to the above aspic and place in Pixie molds, as in Pixie Molds* recipe. Serve on 1-inch rounds of sautéed toast.
SERVES 6

COLD MEAT ASPIC

When you have a buffet party and wish to serve cold sliced chicken or roast beef, cook it the day before. Arrange it on a serving platter. Cover with aspic and decorate with rings of hard-boiled egg white, red pimiento, watercress, slices of truffle, or slices of ripe olive. The aspic will keep the chicken or meat moist in the refrigerator overnight.

SCALLOPS

Mix finely crushed bread crumbs with butter and Grey Poupon Dijon mustard. Bread small bay scallops and broil for a few minutes. Serve on toothpicks.

If you are unable to get bay scallops, cut sea scallops into bite-size pieces.

STUFFED BRUSSELS SPROUTS

Hollow out raw brussels sprouts and fill with cream cheese mixed with ham pâté seasoned with mustard to taste. Place on toothpicks and stick all over a grapefruit so that it resembles a flower. (A small piece should be sliced from the bottom of the grapefruit to seat it firmly.) Surround with sprigs of parsley.

I prefer to blanch brussels sprouts for 3 minutes in boiling water, then strain, dry on paper towels, and proceed as above.

STUFFED NASTURTIUMS

These are delicious with cocktails, for a ladies' luncheon, or around a sandwich platter for tea. Merely stuff nasturtium blossoms with cream cheese, which you have softened with a little cream and to which you have added a little Spice Islands Beau Monde seasoning. Stuffing should be bland, as nasturtiums are tangy.

An amusing anecdote: A letter was received from a woman who had the recipe, asking if she could use plastic nasturtiums.

STUFFED SNOW PEAS

Remove ends and strings from snow peas, blanch for 1 minute in boiling water, strain, and place on paper towels. Using a pastry tube or small spoon, stuff with any soft cheese or cream cheese seasoned with Worcestershire sauce to taste. Refrigerate.

Cherry tomatoes are an attractive and colorful garnish for the serving plate.

WAFFLE CROQUE-MONSIEUR

Take cold baked or boiled ham and sauté in butter. Dry on paper towels, place between 2 pieces of sliced Cheddar cheese, and then between 2 slices of lightly buttered Pepperidge Farm or Arnold's white or Thomas' protein bread (regular-size slices). Butter sandwich on outer sides. Place in preheated waffle iron and toast until crisp. Serve in small squares as hors d'oeuvre or whole with a cheese sauce poured around. This is served as a first course for luncheon or a Sunday night supper.

WATERCRESS RING MOLD

2 cups canned chicken stock
   or broth (remove fat with
   paper towel)
1 shallot or small onion
Juice of 1 lemon
1½ bunches watercress
   leaves
1¾ tablespoons Knox
   unflavored gelatin

2 cups celery root julienne or
   chopped celery
Mayonnaise to taste
Dijon mustard to taste
Cherry tomatoes or sliced
   larger tomatoes
1 bunch watercress or 1
   lettuce

Place 1 cup chicken stock, the shallot, lemon juice, and 1½ bunches watercress leaves in blender and blend for ½ minute. Pour into pan and add ¾ cup chicken stock and softened gelatin, which you have soaked in the remaining ¼ cup of stock. Heat until gelatin is dissolved. Pour into an oiled mold. Place in refrigerator for several hours. Unmold and fill center with chopped celery root julienne, mixed with mayonnaise and Dijon mustard to taste. Surround with small or sliced tomatoes and watercress or lettuce.

Always dip watercress and lettuce in French dressing before using as a garnish.

SERVES 6 TO 8

Soups

Soups:
Hot and Cold

BLACK MUSHROOM SOUP

*(Unusual because it is not only clear
but also thick)*

¾ pound mushrooms
   (preferably the ones that
   are black inside)
3 (10½-ounce) cans
   Campbell's beef broth (or
   2 cans broth, 1 of water)*
3 tablespoons dry French
   vermouth, or to taste

2 tablespoons potato starch
   mixed in ¼ cup cold
   water
Freshly ground pepper to
   taste
Whipped cream (optional)

Clean mushrooms in flour and water (see Mushrooms*). Remove stems, chop caps coarsely, and place in Cuisinart in 2 batches, using off-and-on method, until finely chopped. Cook in the broth for about 15 minutes. Strain broth through fine sieve and return to pan, reserving mushrooms for another use. Add the vermouth and potato starch. Cook to slightly thicken, and season with pepper (no salt!).

* A homemade beef and veal stock of course makes a better soup, if you have the time.

This is one of the soups I serve in pot de crème cups, in the living room, with a teaspoon of whipped cream on top (optional).

Another way to serve at the table is to place the whipped cream on top of the soup and run under broiler to brown, like boula-boula. It will not crack your cups.

SERVES 4 TO 6

The strained, mashed mushroom tops make the best sandwiches, using Pepperidge Farm thin-sliced white bread, a tiny squeeze of lemon on the mushrooms, and salt and pepper. The sandwiches freeze beautifully and can be served plain or toasted. Also, they can be cut into little squares and sautéed in butter to serve with cocktails.

I find that serving soup in pot de crème cups in the living room is helpful to the service of a dinner. Your guests who do not drink are pleased and those who do sometimes find it welcome for a different reason!

BORSCHT SOUP HINT

Pepperidge Farm borscht is excellent. Simply chill and serve with sour cream.

For a hearty luncheon soup, add cut-up hard-boiled eggs and cucumber to the borscht. Serve with a thin toasted bacon and curry mayonnaise sandwich and fruit for dessert.

CLAM BROTH BELLEVUE

(Another soup I serve in the living room)

This hot soup is half chicken stock and half clam juice, with a dash of Worcestershire sauce and with whipped cream on top. Serve in pot de crème cups. Canned chicken broth can be used, but of course homemade is better.

COLD DIET WATERCRESS SOUP

2 envelopes G. Washington
   golden seasoning and broth
1 heaping teaspoon yogurt
3 cups buttermilk
6 tablespoons chopped
   watercress

2 tablespoons cut chives
2 tablespoons chopped fresh
   tarragon

Dissolve the broth in the yogurt, combine with the buttermilk, add the watercress, chives, and tarragon, then chill thoroughly before serving. This makes a delightful warm-weather dish because it is low in calories and can be made with a minimum of effort.

SERVES 4

COLD FRESH TOMATO SOUP

8 large fresh tomatoes
2 medium onions or 12 small
   shallots
½ teaspoon sugar
½ teaspoon Spice Islands
   fines herbes
Juice of 1 lemon

1 tablespoon grated lemon
   rind
Plenty of salt and freshly
   ground pepper to taste
Mayonnaise or sour cream
Curry powder
Chopped parsley

Peel and seed the tomatoes. Put the onions or shallots and the tomatoes in Cuisinart, adding the sugar, fines herbes, lemon juice, lemon rind, salt, and pepper, and chop coarsely, using the knife blade. Chill in refrigerator for 2 hours or longer. About 10 minutes before serving, put the soup in the freezer so that it will be ice-cold before serving.

Serve topped with mayonnaise or sour cream seasoned with curry powder. Garnish with chopped parsley.

An attractive way to serve this and other cold soups is to beat an egg white in a low flat dish, placing rim of empty cups first in egg white and then in finely chopped parsley. Do this ahead and refrigerate until serving time.

All cold soups should be served in refrigerated soup cups.

SERVES 4

COLD LEMON SOUP

This is a quick version of a Greek soup,
but with no cooking.

1 (10¾-ounce) can
  Campbell's cream of
  chicken soup
1 cup cream

1 cup chicken stock
3 tablespoons finely chopped
  mint leaves
Juice of 2 lemons

Strain soup, add the cream, chicken stock, finely chopped mint leaves, and lemon juice. Soup must be served ice-cold.

If you do not have chicken stock, the soup is still good thinned with cream and milk. The soup must not be too thick. Soup cups may be decorated with parsley (see preceding recipe)—this is more effective on glass cups.

SERVES 4

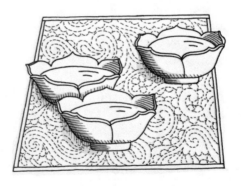

COLD WATERCRESS SOUP

4 cups *canned* chicken stock
    or broth without gelatin
¾ envelope Knox unflavored
    gelatin (or not quite a
    tablespoon)
1 large shallot, peeled

Juice of ½ lemon
1 large bunch watercress,
    leaves only
Salt and pepper to taste
Mayonnaise or sour cream
Horseradish sauce (optional)

Remove any fat on top of contents of can of chicken stock
with a paper towel. Soak gelatin in 1 cup chicken stock. Place
¾ cup chicken stock in blender. Add the shallot, lemon juice,
and watercress leaves. Blend. Pour into a pan with the rest of the
stock and heat. Add the gelatin-stock mixture, stir until dissolved, then add salt and pepper to taste. Place in a bowl and refrigerate for 3 hours or more. When cold and jellied, put in cups
and top with chopped peeled tomatoes with a little mayonnaise
or sour cream, either plain or mixed with a little horseradish
sauce.

This soup is delicious served hot with whipped cream on top.
SERVES 4

GAZPACHO

5 medium ripe tomatoes,
  peeled
2 medium onions, peeled
1 small green pepper, seeded
2 medium cucumbers, peeled
Salt and freshly ground
  pepper to taste
2 tablespoons wine vinegar

5 tablespoons mayonnaise
1 clove garlic, or more
  according to your taste
Finely chopped cucumbers
Chopped pimiento or
  tomatoes
Chopped green pepper
Croutons*

Chop the tomatoes, onions, green pepper, and cucumbers. Put vegetables in a saucepan, add ½ cup cold water (or 1 cup, depending on the juice of the tomatoes), and simmer for about 1 hour. Strain through a sieve, stirring until all the juice is extracted, season with salt and ground pepper to taste, and stir in the wine vinegar. Chill in refrigerator until icy.

In a bowl, combine the mayonnaise and the garlic, forced through a garlic press. Then beat in the icy vegetable juice with a wire whip until mixture looks like a thin, smooth cream soup.

Pass in separate dishes: finely chopped cucumbers with skins on, chopped pimiento or chopped tomatoes, chopped green pepper, and Croutons.

There are many varied recipes for Gazpacho; however, I prefer this old one from the Ritz in Madrid.

An interesting way to serve it is in an extra-large chilled wine goblet.

SERVES 4

EMMIE BERG'S GREEN HORSERADISH SOUP

Cook 2 (10-ounce) boxes Birds Eye deluxe tender tiny frozen peas according to package directions. Place in blender or Cuisinart with 1 peeled, cut-up onion and ½ cup cream and blend. Pour into a saucepan. Add 1 cup chicken stock and more cream to reach desired consistency. Heat. Serve with horseradish whipped cream on top, made with dried, bottled, or freshly grated horseradish to taste. If using fresh horseradish, grate into cream, strain, and then whip. Serve with Croutons*. To serve cold, horseradish may be added directly to the soup and cut-up water chestnuts placed in bottom of cup.

SERVES 4

JACQUELINE CARDELLI'S
LOMBARDIAN BROTH

2 (10½-ounce) cans
Campbell's beef broth,
with Spice Islands fines
herbes (or a mixture of
your own fresh herbs) and
1 tablespoon chopped
parsley added (or equal
measurements of your own
clear beef broth)

1 (8-ounce) liverwurst
sausage
1 egg
¼ to ½ cup fine bread
crumbs

Put broth on to heat, and while you wait, make little liverwurst sausage balls, the size of small marbles. Mash liverwurst in a bowl with a fork, stir in the whole egg, and when mixture is creamy, add enough bread crumbs to make a paste stiff enough to roll into small balls. When the broth is simmering (it should only simmer), drop in the little sausage balls. When they rise to the top, after about 3 to 4 minutes, the soup is ready to serve.

If you freeze crêpes, you can also cut them into strips and add to the broth instead of the sausage balls.

SERVES 4

TOMATO SORBET

(A cold soup)

2 (28-ounce) cans Progresso peeled tomatoes with basil leaf
4 tablespoons grated white onion
Salt and pepper to taste

Curry mayonnaise (I prefer Hellmann's, to which I add a good curry powder to taste, for this particular recipe)
Popadums

Push the tomatoes gently through sieve, as you do not want seeds. Add grated onions, lots of freshly ground pepper, and salt to taste. Place in a covered shallow pan in your freezer. On the day you wish to serve it, cut it up into small pieces and process in Cuisinart, using knife blade, or blender until soft and smooth. Return to freezer.

About 5 or 8 minutes before serving, remove from freezer to soften and place in ice-cold soup cups with 2 heaping tablespoons of curry mayonnaise on top of each. Serve with popadums, an Indian thin, crisp wafer, prepared according to the directions on the tin or package.

SERVES 6

If you have wonderful tomatoes from your garden, or you can buy them, make this sorbet with them, proceeding as above. .

SARA'S QUICK YELLOW
SQUASH SOUP

3 pounds yellow squash
Powdered or cubed chicken
   bouillon sufficient to make
   3 cups soup

6 tablespoons butter

Trim flower and stem ends from the squash and boil the whole squash in 5 quarts of water until tender.

In Cuisinart, using steel knife, purée half the hot squash with half the bouillon powder or cubes and half the butter until completely smooth. Pour into a large serving bowl. Purée the other half of the ingredients in the same way and add to the first half, stirring well to combine thoroughly. Taste for seasoning and correct if necessary. (The chicken cubes are salty.)

This is delicious served hot or cold, and chicken stock can be added to it if you desire.

SERVES 4 TO 6

VIRGINIA'S COLD CAMPBELL'S SOUP

To 2 (10½-ounce) cans Campbell's beef consommé add ¼ cup canned tomato juice, 3 tablespoons lemon juice, 2 tablespoons Worcestershire sauce, and freshly ground pepper to taste. Put in a bowl, and jell for 3 hours or more in refrigerator.

In the bottom of cold soup cup, place any of the following:

1. Peeled tomatoes and celery, chopped fine.
2. Tuna fish, cooked lobster, or crab meat, finely chopped, plain or combined with the tomatoes and celery.

Place soup on top and garnish with 1 heaping tablespoon curry mayonnaise.

SERVES 4

Salads

Salads

QUICK BEET SALAD

Chill 3 cans Pepperidge Farm borscht and strain through a sieve. Combine beets with small pieces of seeded cucumber, adding Cuisinart Mayonnaise* or Hellmann's to taste. Serve over salad greens or toss with the greens.

The strained beet juice from 1 can makes a soup cup of very good cold beet soup with the addition of sour cream, on top or stirred into the juice.

SERVES 6

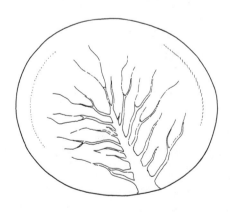

CHEESE BIBB SLICES

Wash small heads of Bibb lettuce well by spraying water into head, keeping it intact. Drain well, stuff paper toweling in between leaves, and roll up in a clean dish towel (I keep a white terry towel for this purpose). Refrigerate. When dry and cold, remove paper and spread any soft cheese of your choice (I prefer Saga, a Danish cheese) on as many leaves as possible.

Wrap each head tightly in a paper towel and place in refrigerator for at least 1 hour. When ready to serve, slice in 1-inch slices (2 or 3 to a person), and pour a tart French dressing over them.

HEARTS OF PALM WITH
WATERCRESS DRESSING

Place 1 bunch (leaves only) of watercress and ¾ cup My French Dressing* in blender (if bunch is not large, use 1½ bunches). Dressing should be thick and green. Place over 1 can hearts of palm sliced lengthwise or canned celery hearts.

This dressing is also good on celery root, cooked or canned.

SERVES 4

MARY'S SALAD

2 large or 4 small Bibb lettuces	6 strips bacon
¼ cup minced shallots	1 egg
1 teaspoon granulated sugar	¼ cup vinegar
Salt and freshly ground black pepper to taste	½ cup water

Break up lettuce, and toss with shallots, sugar, and seasonings. Keep refrigerated.

Meanwhile fry bacon and, when crisp, drain on paper towels. Pour off most of fat from pan. Beat egg slightly with vinegar and water and mix well. Break bacon into small pieces. Cook egg mixture slowly in fat left in pan, stirring all the while. (Egg must be slightly runny.) Let cool a little, pour over lettuce, sprinkle with bacon, and toss well.

SERVES 4

RICE SALAD

1½ cups long-grain rice
3 medium tomatoes, plus 1
large tomato for petals
½ (10-ounce) box frozen
peas
4 stalks celery
1 cucumber

½ cup chopped parsley
1 teaspoon Spice Islands fines
herbes (or fresh herbs of
your choice)
Salt and pepper to taste
My French Dressing*
1 bunch watercress

Cook rice according to the directions in the recipe for Fluffy Rice*. Scald and skin the 3 medium tomatoes, quarter, and remove seeds. Cook peas and refresh (by rinsing with cold water) until quite cold. Slice celery and peel and dice cucumber. Mix vegetables with rice, adding the chopped parsley, fines herbes, and salt and pepper to taste. Stir in the French dressing, press into a 1-quart ring mold, and place in refrigerator. When cold, turn out on a round platter, fill center of ring mold with sprigs of watercress dipped in French dressing, and decorate top of rice with Tomato Petals* brushed with French dressing.

If you are serving the ring mold for a buffet, the center may be filled with crab meat or chicken salad.

SERVES 6

Any one of these salads makes a main course for luncheon, served on a large plate (I use $11\frac{1}{2}$-inch plates with no border). The directions given are for each plate, or individual serving.

POTATO SALAD AND SLICED BEEF

A Hearty Salad

Potato Shrimp Mold*, made with 4 medium boiled potatoes, 16 medium shrimps or 8 large cut in half, and a few peas
4 hard-boiled eggs, boiled in Campbell's beef broth
Curry mayonnaise

16 paper-thin slices of cold beef of your choice
$\frac{1}{2}$ pound green beans
1 large tomato
16 snow peas
$\frac{1}{2}$ recipe Carrots Estragon*, puréed
4 radishes

For each serving: individual Potato Shrimp Mold; a sliced hard-boiled egg on curried mayonnaise; 4 slices steak, fillet, or roast beef; a bunch of Green Beans* with Tomato Petals* overlapping; 4 snow peas (remove ends and strings, blanch in boiling water for 1 minute, and plunge into ice water) filled with purée of Carrots Estragon by piping with small pastry tube, and decorated with a radish rose. Serve with toasted Pita Bread*.

SERVES 4

ARTICHOKE MOUGINS

Prepare 4 artichokes according to Artichokes (Basic Recipe)*, adding 1 clove garlic and 1 tablespoon oil. When they are cooked and drained, clean out the center of each artichoke. Use a knife to make a circular cut inside the center of the artichoke, then use a spoon to remove the choke, leaving the heart and outer leaves intact. There will be a well in the center when you are through.

Fill the cleaned-out center with a portion of the following salad: cook 4 ears of corn and cut off kernels. Clean, devein, and cook ¼ pound raw shrimp. Cut into small pieces. Mix 1 cup cooked green peas with corn and shrimp and fold in mayonnaise, seasoned to taste. Fill artichoke center.

Decorate the artichoke to make it look like a large flower by placing equally thin slices of lemon, hard-boiled egg, and tomato in between the rows of artichoke leaves.

Prepare decoration as follows: zest a lemon vertically with equidistant spaces between zests. Slice lemon horizontally in slices about ⅛ inch thick. Slice hard-boiled eggs in the egg slicer. Slice a medium tomato horizontally.

Layer the vegetables between the leaves, starting with a row of lemons, then tomatoes, and finally hard-boiled eggs. Put a slice of tomato and one of hard-boiled egg in the center of the artichoke, on top of the salad.

This is a perfect main course for luncheon. Menu suggestion: Black Mushroom Soup* served in pot de crème cups in the living room; Artichoke Mougins; buttered pita bread; and Apricot Soufflé*.

SERVES 4

BIBB LETTUCE FLOWER

Select 4 equally small heads of Bibb lettuce, allowing 1 head per person. Gently wash the head, running cold water between all of the leaves while keeping the leaves intact and attached. Turn the head upside down and drain, then squeeze gently. Put paper towels between as many leaves as possible, wrap in a towel, and place in the refrigerator.

Sauté 4 pounded chicken breasts in a very little clarified butter, approximately 3 minutes on each side. Allow the breast to cool (do not put in the refrigerator), then slice into long finger strips.

Remove lettuce from refrigerator and discard paper towels.

Mix 1 cup mayonnaise with finely chopped Major Grey's chutney to taste. With a spoon (or a large open-tipped pastry bag), put mayonnaise at the base of each lettuce leaf. Place chicken fingers in the same leaves, securing them in the mayonnaise.

SERVES 4

OPTIONAL: For a more colorful dish, fill the leaves with tomato and/or hard-boiled egg slices, as in Artichoke Mougins*. Any other meat, cut in strips, can be substituted for the sautéed chicken breast.

MENU SUGGESTION: Clam Broth Bellevue*; Bibb Lettuce Flower; French bread or popovers; and for dessert, hot fruit served with Mary Applequist's Cornflake Cookies*.

You can sauté chicken strips as in the Chicken Strips with Mango Sauce* recipe, when you are making chicken salad, in a small amount of clarified butter, then cut into squares and add mayonnaise, celery, grapes, or whatever mixture you prefer. This gives the salad a better flavor than when it has been refrigerated for hours.

HEARTS OF PALM, SALMON MOUSSE, AND SHRIMP

2 (8-ounce) cans hearts of
   palm
My French Dressing*
24 cooked large shrimps
1 bunch watercress
1 large whole cucumber,
   peeled, seeds removed with
   a long corer, and cut into
   ½-inch rings

1 (7¼-ounce) can salmon or
   1 (¼-inch) slice fresh
   salmon
2 medium tomatoes
A few branches fresh basil,
   chopped
2 hard-boiled eggs

Two rolls of canned hearts of palm marinated in French dressing with 3 cooked shrimps curved over top of each roll for decoration, spread watercress on plate, place on it 3 cucumber rings filled with cold Salmon Mousse* (prepared according to the instructions for Shrimp Mousse on page 169) to resemble a flower, tomato slices with chopped fresh basil on top and French dressing, and half of a hard-boiled and stuffed egg (yolk mixed with mayonnaise and seasoning of your choice). Serve with a buttered Flour Tortilla*.

SERVES 4

CURRIED COTTAGE CHEESE AND FRUITS

1 (12-ounce) container
  cottage cheese, regular or
  low-fat
Curry powder to taste
10 slices crisp-cooked bacon

Fresh fruits
Salad greens
My French Dressing*
Mayonnaise with chopped
  mango chutney

Serve curried cottage cheese (mix curry powder to taste into cottage cheese of your choice) with crisp crumbled bacon on top, all kinds of fresh fruits, making a decorative arrangement, plus salad greens and French dressing (or dressing of your choice) and chutney mayonnaise. Serve with Melba Toast* made with Thomas' protein bread.

SERVES 4

CHICKEN PESTO

4 chicken breasts
Pesto Sauce*
Noodles
Assorted cooked vegetables
4 sliced tomatoes
1 avocado

My French Dressing*
1 Stouffer's French bread
    pizza (½ package),
    toasted and sliced into
    small slices

Prepare the chicken breasts according to the recipe for Chicken Strips with Mango Sauce*, sauté, and cool. For each serving, place chicken strips with Pesto Sauce on the side, adding 1 portion of noodles with assorted cooked vegetables (noodles primavera), alternate slices of tomato and avocado with French dressing, and 2 slices toasted pizza.

SERVES 4

Luncheon
Dishes

Luncheon Dishes

ARTICHOKE BOTTOMS WITH CRAB MEAT MOUSSELINE

4 artichoke bottoms, fresh or
canned
8 heaping tablespoons crab
meat

Mousseline Sauce* or
Hollandaise Sauce*

Fresh artichoke bottoms are preferable, but you can use canned imported artichoke bottoms, rinsing well and squeezing lemon over them. Warm in a steamer or sauté. Place a mound of crab meat on top, cover with Mousseline Sauce or Hollandaise Sauce and run under the broiler (with rack in the middle) until hot and glazed.

This makes a wonderful first course for luncheon. I decorate the plate with 6 or 7 unscraped artichoke leaves with the ends embedded in the sauce, ready to eat.

If making 6 of these, I assemble the crab meat on the artichoke bottoms and place them in a steamer to keep warm. They may be held for 10 minutes. At serving time, cover with Mousseline and run under the broiler.

SERVES 4

Any of the Nouvelle Cuisine Salads (pages 71–76) with Melba Toast* or Paper-thin Toasted Sandwich*, and for dessert, Irish coffee but made with Kahlúa and a small amount of either whipped cream or Cool Whip on top, with Mary Applequist's Cornflake Cookies*.

Virginia's Cold Campbell's Soup* and a Paper-thin Toasted Sandwich* of curry mayonnaise and bacon. For dessert, Strawberry Cinnamon Toasts*, melon, or fresh fruit with Fruit Sauce*.

QUICK BRIDGE LUNCHEON FOR FOUR

My friend Julia W. hates to cook and plays the best bridge! Here is her quick luncheon before the game.

4 hard-boiled eggs
½ cup cream
1 (10¾-ounce) can
    Campbell's cream of
    mushroom soup
¼ pound fresh mushrooms,
    thinly sliced

1 tablespoon tomato paste
1 teaspoon curry powder, or
    to taste
¼ pound cooked shrimp
Pepperidge Farm
    herb-seasoned stuffing

Slice hard-boiled eggs in half. Place in a casserole with the cream, mushroom soup, mushrooms, tomato paste, curry powder to taste, and shrimp. Stir to mix well and top with buttered Pepperidge Farm stuffing. Bake, uncovered, in a preheated 350° F. oven until hot and top is brown, about 10 minutes.

LUNCHEON: Cold soup, sometimes! Egg dish. A green salad with toasted English muffins. No dessert. Bridge!

CHEESE SOUFFLÉ

3 tablespoons butter
3 tablespoons all-purpose
  flour
1 cup milk
Salt and pinch of cayenne
  pepper to taste
4 egg yolks
1 cup grated sharp Cheddar
  cheese, preferably
  imported, or Gruyère

1 tablespoon Worcestershire
  sauce
1 scant teaspoon dry mustard
  or prepared mustard
6 egg whites, stiffly beaten

Tie a wax-paper collar around a 1-quart soufflé dish or casserole. The collar should come 2 inches above the top of the dish. I use wire ties from the garden, such as "Twist-ems," instead of string or paper clips. Much quicker!

Melt the butter in a saucepan over medium heat. Stir in the flour and blend well for at least 5 minutes. Pour in the milk and season with the salt and cayenne. Remove the saucepan from the fire and beat in the egg yolks, one at a time, alternately with the grated cheese. Stir the mixture until the cheese has melted. Add the Worcestershire sauce and mustard. When all the ingredients are well blended, cool slightly. Fold in stiffly beaten egg whites and pour the batter into the generously buttered soufflé dish or casserole. Bake in a preheated 375° F. (moderate) oven for about 35 minutes, or until the top is delicately browned. Serve at once.

SERVES 4 OR 5

ARTICHOKES WITH CHEESE SOUFFLÉ

(A suggestion from a friend)

Cook 4 artichokes as in Basic Recipe*, only be very careful to undercook a little bit. Hollow out center of artichokes, remove prickly leaves, and clean right down to the top of artichoke bottom. Tie each artichoke with a string to hold leaves upright, or you can use a wax-paper collar tied with garden "Twist-ems."

Preheat oven to 450° F. Fill cooked artichokes with Cheese Soufflé*. Place on a buttered cookie sheet in oven and bake until soufflé puffs up, about 12 to 15 minutes. Remove collar or string and pass Sauce Quo Vadis (recipe follows) to pour over the artichokes. This sauce comes from the Quo Vadis Restaurant in New York, where it is served with individual cheese soufflés, in which a hole is made in the center into which to pour the sauce when served.

SERVES 4

Sauce Quo Vadis*

3 or 4 shallots, peeled and finely chopped
2 tablespoons red wine vinegar
1 teaspoon Dijon mustard
⅓ cup Escoffier sauce Robert
1 cup chicken broth, your own or canned condensed
¼ cup heavy cream

Combine the shallots and vinegar in a saucepan and cook over moderate heat until almost all the vinegar has evaporated. Stir in all remaining ingredients thoroughly. Bring to a boil, reduce heat, and simmer for about 6 minutes, or until the sauce has thickened slightly. Strain. Taste for seasoning. Pour into a heated sauceboat.

* Quo Vadis is one of the best and oldest restaurants in New York City—under the same management since 1946!

CRUSTY LUNCHEON CHEESE

1 stale 1-pound loaf sliced white Pepperidge Farm bread
¼ pound melted butter (clarified), plus butter for dish
½ pound Cheddar cheese, grated
4 eggs, slightly beaten

2 cups light cream
¼ cup milk
1 teaspoon salt
¼ teaspoon paprika
Few grains cayenne pepper
¼ teaspoon Dijon mustard
1 teaspoon Worcestershire sauce
½ pound bacon (optional)

This is a quiche without the pastry crust. Preheat oven to 350° F. (moderate). Butter a shallow baking dish. Trim crusts from bread. Cut so the bread will stand 1½ inches above height of dish. Spread bread with melted butter on both sides. Fit slices together around sides and bottom of dish. Tie buttered waxpaper collar around outside of dish to hold up bread. Cover bottom layer with the grated cheese. Combine all the other ingredients except the bacon, and pour over cheese. Bake 30 minutes in moderate oven. Take out and sprinkle with crisp bacon, finely crumbled (optional).

SERVES 6

SIMCA'S INDIVIDUAL CHEESE SOUFFLÉS WITH TARRAGON CREAM SAUCE

2½ tablespoons butter for ramekins

5 level tablespoons all-purpose flour, tapped to settle

1 cup cold milk

Salt

Black pepper, freshly ground

Nutmeg, freshly ground

3 egg yolks

4 egg whites

½ cup grated Swiss cheese

(*Recommended equipment:* 12 half-cup ramekins or timbale molds.)

Heavily butter the ramekins or timbale molds and set them in the refrigerator to chill until they are to be used.

Make the bouillie: Put the flour into an enameled saucepan and very gradually add the cold milk, a little at a time, stirring with a whisk or spatula to make a smooth paste. Pour in the remaining milk and stir thoroughly. Add a pinch of salt and season highly with pepper and nutmeg. Set over medium heat and stir continuously for several minutes until the mixture is quite smooth and thick. Remove from the heat and continue to stir for a few seconds to cool the bouillie slightly. Set aside.

Separate 4 eggs, dropping the whites into a mixing bowl and 3 of the yolks, one by one, into the warm bouillie, stirring to incorporate each yolk thoroughly before adding the next.

Beat the egg whites with a pinch of salt until they are stiff but not dry. If the bouillie has cooled, return it to the heat and warm it gently (it should be warmed only enough so that you can still put your finger into it). Then fold it into the stiffly beaten egg whites gradually, sprinkling on the grated cheese at the same time.

To cook the soufflés: Preheat oven to 375° F. Fill the ramekins or timbale molds two-thirds full of the soufflé mixture. Set them in a shallow pan and pour water into the pan to come two thirds of the way up the sides of the molds. Bring the water to a simmer on top of the stove. Then very carefully set the pan with the molds into the preheated oven to cook the soufflés for 12 to 15 minutes, until they have risen a good ¾ inch above the edges of the molds. (The water in the pan must not boil; if it does, regulate the oven temperature.)

When you remove the soufflés from the oven they will deflate a little, but do not worry. They may be served immediately, or they may be held for 24 hours or more before serving. If held, reheat in a bain-marie for 6 to 8 minutes in 350° F. oven.

SERVES 6

Tarragon Cream Sauce

Twenty minutes before serving the soufflés, butter a flat oven-proof dish and unmold the soufflés upside down onto the dish. Prepare the sauce.

1½ to 2 cups heavy cream	Salt
3 to 4 tablespoons fresh tarragon, minced (if dried, use less)	Pepper, freshly ground

Bring the cream to a boil with the tarragon and seasoning and let it simmer slowly for several minutes until it takes on the taste of the tarragon. Pour the boiling sauce over and around the soufflés and return them to the oven for 10 to 12 minutes, or until they swell and absorb almost all the cream.

Serve immediately in the baking dish.

Of all of Simca's wonderful recipes, this is probably my favorite!

CUCUMBER AND SHAD ROE

(This is good for a main luncheon course)

Simmer 4 medium-small cucumbers (as near the length of the shad roe as possible), for 10 to 15 minutes, or until just tender. Cut in half lengthwise, scoop out the seeds, and invert on paper towels to drain. Keep warm. Sauté 1 can shad roe (canned is almost as good as the fresh) in butter until browned on both sides. Place a "fillet" of shad roe in each cucumber cavity and cover with Hollandaise Sauce.*

Fresh crab meat, lobster, or any cooked fish may be used instead of shad roe.

SERVES 4

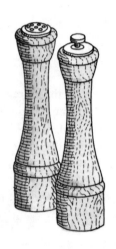

CURRIED EGGS AU BON GOÛT

¼ pound butter
1 large onion, minced
1 heaping tablespoon curry
  powder, plus about 1
  teaspoon
1 scant tablespoon
  all-purpose flour

½ cup consommé
½ cup light cream, plus
  cream for egg yolks
4 hard-boiled eggs, sliced
  lengthwise
Curried Rice*
Finely chopped parsley

First: Melt the butter in a skillet. Sauté the onion, stirring occasionally. Be careful not to allow onion to get too dark in color. Stir in the curry powder and flour. Using wire whisk, continue to stir until smooth.

Second: Blend in the ½ cup consommé, a little at a time. Then add the cream, stirring until sauce thickens.

Third: Mash the hard-boiled egg yolks, add cream to soften, curry powder to taste (start with 1 teaspoon, then taste), and a dash of salt. Fill the whites with this mixture. Stick the two halves together to give the appearance of whole eggs. For each serving, make a round nest of the curried rice with an indentation the size of an egg in the center. Place an egg in it. Cover with the curry sauce and garnish with a ring of finely chopped parsley around the egg.

Serve with Major Grey's chutney.

SERVES 4

EGGS AU BON GOÛT

(A quickie cold egg course for luncheon)

For each serving, sauté a round of dried or stale Pepperidge Farm bread in butter until golden on both sides. Spread with black or red caviar. Cut a thin slice from the bottom of a hard-boiled egg so that the egg will stand upright and place it on the caviar. Cover with a sauce made by reducing fresh or canned tomatoes with onion, basil, butter, and a pinch of sugar, until a thick paste; then strain and add enough to sour cream to give it taste and color. (The unused tomato purée can be frozen for future use.) For a quicker sauce, add ketchup to sour cream.

Since caviar has become so expensive, you may wish to substitute a spread of tuna fish, canned salmon, pâté, or sardines.

FRIZZLED HAM

1½ pounds baked ham
2½ tablespoons butter

½ cup light or dark brown
sugar

Ask your butcher to slice cold baked ham on the thinnest slicer, as for dried beef. Separate the slices and shred them into pieces. Melt the butter in a heavy frying pan (preferably a black cast-iron one) and sauté the ham for about 8 minutes, or until it begins to crisp, stirring constantly with a fork. Spread the ham on paper towels to remove some of the fat. Return the ham to the pan, sprinkle with the brown sugar, and cook for about 6 minutes longer. Place on cookie sheet and crisp even more in a preheated 250° F. oven.

Use sautéed ham as a border for the following dishes:
1. Creamed crab meat
2. Creamed chicken or turkey
3. Curried hard-boiled eggs
4. Eggs goldenrod (creamed sliced whites of hard-boiled eggs, the yolks sieved and sprinkled on top)
5. Gnocchi
6. For a salad course, pass sautéed ham with tossed greens and serve with Camembert in aspic.

Cold sliced boiled ham can no longer be prepared this way. It will not become crisp, because of the increased water content; hence, baked ham or dried beef.

But oh, if you are in France, any ham is perfect—no water!

GNOCCHI WITH MORNAY SAUCE

Cuisinart Pâte à Choux
(Cream Puffs)

¼ pound butter
1 cup hot water
1 cup all-purpose flour, sifted
4 eggs
¼ cup grated sharp Cheddar
  cheese

¼ cup grated Parmesan or
  Cheddar cheese, for
  topping

Place butter and water in a heavy pan over medium heat until butter melts. When the butter-water mixture comes to a boil, add the flour all at once and stir with a wooden spoon until dough forms a ball and pulls away from side of pan. Place it at once in the Cuisinart, using steel blade, and blend for about 12 seconds. With motor running, add eggs one at a time. Process until shiny and smooth, adding ¼ cup Cheddar cheese at the end.

Place a roasting pan over two burners and fill halfway with water. When the water simmers, warm 2 teaspoons in a small bowl of hot water and shove off teaspoons of dough into water, cleaning spoons off each time in the hot water. When the gnocchi rise to the top and are springy to the touch, they are done. Remove with slotted spoon to paper towels. When they are all done, place in a shallow buttered casserole and cover with Mornay Sauce (recipe follows), sprinkle with freshly grated Parmesan or Cheddar cheese, and place in preheated 350° F. oven for 20 minutes until hot, bubbly, and brown on top. Place briefly under broiler if not brown enough.

SERVES 6—MAKES 18 TO 20 GNOCCHI

NOTE: This recipe can be made ahead of time and can also be frozen.

Another interesting way to serve is to poach the gnocchi in buttered Pyrex cups in simmering water. When firm and springy, invert on a fried tomato slice the same size as Pyrex cup and cover with Mornay Sauce (recipe follows).

Mornay Sauce

4 tablespoons butter
4 tablespoons all-purpose flour
2 cups milk
2 cups half-and-half
¼ teaspoon Grey Poupon Dijon mustard
3 tablespoons Worcestershire sauce

1 tablespoon fresh onion juice
1 cup grated sharp Cheddar cheese (preferably New York State)
½ cup milk or light cream, if needed to thin the sauce
Salt to taste

Melt the butter, and the flour, and stir with wire whip, then add the 2 cups milk, the half-and-half, mustard, Worcestershire sauce, onion juice, and cheese. Stir until right consistency. If necessary, add ½ cup milk or cream to thin down. Add salt at the last, to taste. Pour the sauce over the gnocchi.

This recipe is delicious with a green salad, melba toast, and a fruit dessert for luncheon; or, for a Sunday night supper, add a border of Frizzled Ham*.

EMMIE BERG'S FLÄSKPANNKAKA

(Swedish Omelette)

4 slices salt pork
1 cup milk, plus milk for
   soaking pork
3 eggs

2 tablespoons all-purpose
   flour
¼ teaspoon salt
Dash of white pepper

Soak salt pork in milk for an hour or more, drain, and cut into tiny squares. Fry until crisp in black cast-iron skillet and set aside. Beat the eggs with rotary beater until light and fluffy, about 4 minutes (less for an electric beater). Add flour a little at a time, beating after each addition. Reheat the skillet and pour off a little fat if it looks like too much. Add seasoning and milk to the eggs, beat, and pour into the hot skillet over the salt pork.

Preheat the oven to 375° F. (moderate). Bake for about 35 minutes, or until puffed, slightly brown, and firm in the center. Slide out onto a hot platter, without folding, and serve with lingonberry preserves or cranberry sauce.

This is good as an entrée for luncheon, followed by a cold meat or fish in aspic, salad, and a hot fruit dessert.

SERVES 4

PAPER-THIN TOASTED SANDWICH

(One slice instead of two!)

Take a regular-size slice of Thomas' protein or Pepperidge Farm or Arnold's white bread, and toast.

Place a folded paper napkin over the toast and slice horizontally through with a serrated knife. (This can be done only while toast is hot!)

Butter the inside of the 2 pieces and place any desired filling in between.

You can reheat in the toaster, completing the sandwich with any of the following:

1. A thin, pounded piece of chuck steak, sautéed until just pink.

2. A thin piece of fillet (naturally, the fillet is more tender), sautéed until just pink.

3. Cooked chicken, with or without mayonnaise.

4. Tuna fish, or any cooked fish, with mayonnaise.

5. Cooked mushrooms.

6. Ham and cheese.

7. Bacon with curry mayonnaise.

This thin sandwich is perfect to serve with a nouvelle cuisine salad for luncheon.

Pepperidge Farm's thin-sliced bread can be sliced in this way.

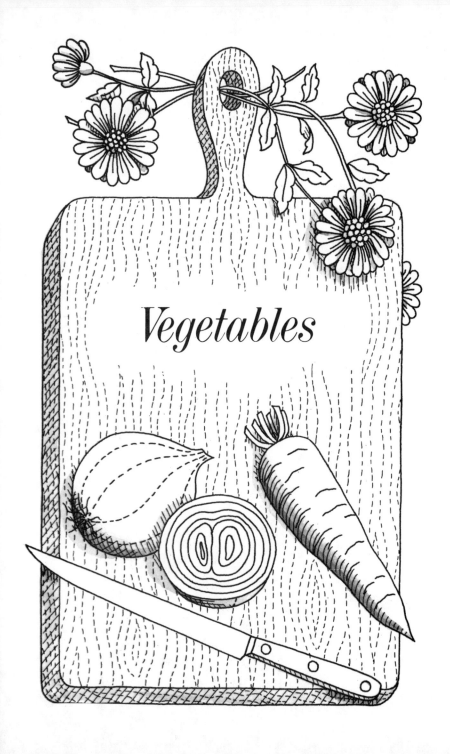

Vegetables

Vegetables, Potatoes, Rice, Soufflés

ARTICHOKES

(Basic Recipe)

Remove the tough or discolored outer leaves from well-rinsed artichokes. Cut off stems and save. Trim all points of leaves with scissors, cut an X in the bottom, rub all over with lemon, and add juice of 1 lemon to the cooking water. Cook in an enamel pan (if you do 6, a shallow enamel roasting pan is perfect, placed over 2 burners). Cover tops of artichokes with a double thickness of cheesecloth and weigh down with a cookie rack or round steamer for rice; otherwise, tie cheesecloth to the handles of the pan. Cook, uncovered, with boiling water almost to the top of the pan, for about 40 to 45 minutes, depending on the size and age. Test for doneness after about 20 minutes by pulling an outer leaf. If it comes away easily, the artichoke is done.

NOTE: Peel stems and cook with the artichokes. These can then be cut up and used with scraped artichokes.

The hint for cooking artichokes in a roasting pan comes from Maurice Moore-Betty.

SCRAPED ARTICHOKES MOUSSELINE

Cook artichokes as in basic recipe, allowing 1 artichoke per person. Remove choke and scrape all leaves. Place all that you have scraped on artichoke bottom. Steam to heat them, cover with Mousseline Sauce*, and run under broiler until light brown. This is delicious as a first course or around filet mignon.

You can make a beautiful salad by arranging the scraped artichoke on the artichoke bottom and decorating with chopped hard-boiled egg whites, with the yolk, sieved, on top.

The scrapings may also be mixed with small pieces of chopped ham and cooked mushroom, sprinkled with bread crumbs and cheese, and browned under the broiler.

GREEN BEANS

Slice string beans lengthwise into thin strips and tie in bunches with string. (Each bunch will be an average-size serving.) Cut the ends so they are even. Place the bunches in ice water for about 30 minutes and then put them in a strainer and run very hot water over them so that they are really hot before plunging them into rapidly boiling water (I use a lot). Boil rapidly until beans are just tender. Always cook in an uncovered pan. Drain. Add butter, salt, pepper, and, if desired, a pinch of thyme.

The following are four interesting ways of serving them:

1. Place bunch of beans on a slice of fried eggplant, discard string, and cover beans with Hollandaise Sauce*, as a first course for a luncheon or dinner.

2. Substitute fried sliced tomatoes, either red or green, for the eggplant—1 slice per serving.

3. When wax beans are in the market, cook bunches of half green and half wax. When done, drain and serve in a long, even row on a platter, pouring melted butter over them and topping them all down the center with buttered croutons.

4. If you are serving quite a few people, an easy way is to put the beans in a shallow casserole, cover with Mousseline Sauce*, and heat at the last moment under the broiler, first on a low rack to warm, then on an upper rack to brown.

If you cook beans ahead of time, after cooking rinse with cold water and drain. Reheat in butter or just in boiling water for a few seconds. I use an oblong asparagus cooker with rack.

BEETS IN MAYONNAISE

Method 1. Cook beets until done (small garden ones are the best tasting, but canned beets may also be used). Slice, return to pan, and heat. Add to the pan just enough mayonnaise, to which you have added tarragon vinegar as you would a squeeze of lemon juice, to coat the beets.

Method 2. Cook beets as above; then dice small and heat. Stir in mayonnaise and place in a well or ring of hot chopped spinach. (Delicious with baked ham.)

CAVIAR CAULIFLOWER

(For a buffet)

Cook and drain a large head of cauliflower. Chill thoroughly. Arrange whole on a bed of greens and cover with the following sauce:

1 cup sour cream
1 tablespoon finely chopped
    shallots or onions
2 teaspoons capers

4 tablespoons red caviar
Pepper to taste
3 tablespoons chopped
    parsley

Combine the ingredients and let stand for 1 hour before pouring over the chilled cauliflower.
SERVES 6 TO 8

GREEN CAULIFLOWER WITH CROUTONS

Clean cauliflower and insert sharp knife into core, from bottom, making an X. Place lemon slices (lemon keeps cauliflower white) to cover top and tie in cheesecloth. Boil in salted water for 25 to 45 minutes, according to size of cauliflower. While this is cooking, prepare 2 (10-ounce) boxes Birds Eye tiny frozen peas as directed on package, adding 1 medium sliced onion. Drain and place peas in blender or Cuisinart with 1 tablespoon of butter and ¼ cup light cream (optional). Blend until it becomes purée. (My grandson, who is a chef, processes the peas in the Cuisinart and then in the blender to achieve a very fine purée.) Add salt and pepper to taste. Drain cauliflower well, having removed cheesecloth and lemon. Keep purée very hot, adding a little more cream if necessary. Coat cauliflower with the purée and dot with sautéed croutons or tiny cherry tomatoes.

To serve 6, use a larger cauliflower.

SERVES 4 TO 6

CARROTS ESTRAGON

2 bunches small carrots
2 tablespoons butter
¼ scant teaspoon sugar
2 or 3 lettuce leaves
2 tablespoons chopped
　parsley

1 tablespoon chopped fresh
　tarragon or 1 teaspoon
　dried tarragon
¼ teaspoon salt
⅛ teaspoon pepper

Scrub carrots with a stiff brush and slice thinly, or julienne. Into a frying pan, put butter and sugar. Add carrots, then cover with lettuce leaves dripping with water. Cover pan and cook over low heat 20 minutes. Take out lettuce. Add parsley, tarragon, salt, and pepper. Mix well and serve immediately in a hot dish.

The lettuce may be served with the carrots, by arranging it on one side to look attractive, as lettuce prepared in this manner is very tasty.

This method of steaming carrots I use for purée, with or without the lettuce, and adding a pinch of nutmeg. Serve topped with snow peas (optional).

SERVES 6

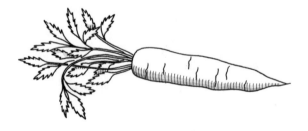

CELERY ROOT FIVE WAYS

You can buy very good imported celery root in a can; strain it in a sieve and run water over it. Allow 1 large slice per person. Steam it until hot or even put it on a platter in the oven to warm. If you wish to really cook it yourself, take a raw celery root, peel, slice about ½ inch thick, and steam (I use Wearever's Bungalow Cooker or steamer) or boil in water until barely soft (should be a little crisp).

Method 1. Place warm celery root slices on an ovenproof platter and top with chopped, creamed mushrooms to which you have added dry French vermouth to taste. Very good with steak.

Method 2. Place hot Purée of Peas* on top, sprinkle with Parmesan cheese, and run under broiler.

Method 3. Place hot chopped cooked spinach on top. Make a well in the center of the spinach with a soup spoon and fill with Mousseline Sauce.* Run under the broiler until golden brown on top.

Method 4. Use canned or cooked cold celery root slices. Make a watercress dressing in your blender as follows: For 6 people, place ¼ cup of My French Dressing* in blender. Add the leaves only of 1 bunch of watercress. Blend. Add ½ cup more of French dressing and pour this green dressing over cold celery root, sliced tomatoes, or a small individual head of Bibb lettuce, which you then dot with cherry tomatoes to look like a flower. This dressing is also good over hearts of palm.

Method 5. Place crab meat, which you have heated in the top of a double boiler, on top of heated slice of celery root, preferably fresh, and cover with Hollandaise Sauce*. Serve as a main course for luncheon, adding cooked asparagus tips if you wish.

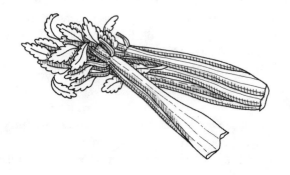

BRAISED CELERY

Chop 3 carrots and 3 shallots, place in pan, and add 1 tablespoon butter. Cook, covered, over medium until done. Drain off butter. Place on bottom of a shallow baking dish. Drain 1 can celery hearts and slice hearts in half lengthwise. Place on top of carrots and cover with sauce made as follows:

Add 2½ tablespoons potato starch to 1 (10½-ounce) can Campbell's beef consommé, cook until thickened, add 2 tablespoons glace de viande (optional) and a squeeze of lemon. If sauce is too thick, add a little more consommé.

Preheat oven to 350° F. Bake until hot.

SERVES 6

BRAISED BIBB LETTUCE OR CELERY
AU BON GOÛT

Allow 2 small heads of Bibb lettuce per person. Wash and trim heads. Place heads in uncovered pot of boiling water, with pinch of baking soda, for 2 minutes only. Squeeze very gently between paper towels to remove liquid. Arrange heads around edge of buttered shallow baking dish, working inward so that heads make a design. Season with salt and pepper.

Preheat oven to 425° F. Pour the following sauce over Bibb, just covering each one. Place dish in oven for about 5 minutes, or just long enough to be sure it is hot. Lettuce must be firm and green, not overcooked.

Sauce Au Bon Goût for Braised Bibb or Celery

Put 1 tablespoon of butter in pan, melt, and add 2 good teaspoons potato starch. Stir in 1 (10½-ounce) can of Campbell's beef consommé and add 1 tablespoon of glace de viande (optional), a squeeze of lemon, and salt and white pepper to taste. Cook until thick and clear.

NOTE: This sauce is delicious with canned celery hearts, which are sliced in half lengthwise. Pour off juice in a 12-ounce can, rinse celery, and cover with above sauce, baking 20 minutes or more. This serves 6.

CUCUMBER RINGS

Wash and peel 6 cucumbers with striper to make stripes. Cut 1½ inches thick (crosswise). Scoop out seeds with a spoon, place cucumber rings in a shallow pan and sprinkle over 2 tablespoons wine vinegar, 1½ teaspoons salt, and ⅛ teaspoon sugar. Let stand for at least 30 minutes. Drain carefully and pat dry with paper towels.

Preheat oven to 375° F. Place cucumber rings in shallow baking dish with 3 tablespoons melted butter, ⅓ teaspoon dill or basil, 3 or 4 tablespoons minced green onions, and ⅛ teaspoon pepper. Cook for about 25 minutes, or until tender but still crisp.

SERVES 6

These can be served in one of the following ways:

1. Around a fish dish, filling center with fish sauce sprinkled with parsley.

2. Filled with Hollandaise Sauce* and served around a broiled fish.

3. Soubise Sauce (page 156).

4. With tomatoes and bread crumbs on top.

5. If you wish these as a main course, spread shallow baking dish with Hollandaise Sauce*, top with cucumber rings filled with creamed fish, and sprinkle with chopped parsley.

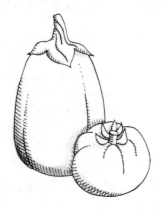

EGGPLANT SHOREACRES

1 eggplant
2 large tomatoes
Salt and pepper

⅓ recipe Hollandaise Sauce*
⅔ recipe Béchamel Sauce*

Preheat oven to 350° F. Peel and slice eggplant and tomatoes ½ inch thick. Sprinkle with salt and pepper. Place eggplant on tomato and put on a flat baking dish. Cover with aluminum foil and bake about 20 minutes. Hold over sink and drain all juice from under the foil, then remove foil. (The cooked eggplant and tomatoes can be kept warm in oven until ready for sauce at serving time.)

Cover with sauce made of one-third Hollandaise and two-thirds Béchamel. Place under broiler until lightly browned.

If you wish a main luncheon dish, space bunches of tied Green Beans* on top of lightly browned sauce.

SERVES 4

PURÉE OF PEAS
AND VARIOUS WAYS TO SERVE IT

1. Cook 2 (10-ounce) boxes, or more, of frozen peas according to instructions on box, adding 1 medium onion cut into pieces. While still warm, purée in the Cuisinart, adding salt and pepper to taste and a tablespoon of cream if desired. This purée may be made ahead of time. I always make extra to freeze, so I will have it on hand for making Emmie Berg's Green Horseradish Soup*, to place on artichoke bottoms, inside a tomato, or on cooked celery root, or to decorate a platter of meat.

2. Sauté 6 mushrooms, which you have cut up, then place in Cuisinart with your peas. Open 2 cans of imported artichoke bottoms, remove from can, rinse, and drain; or, if available, use freshly cooked ones. When ready to serve, sauté or steam artichoke bottoms until hot. Place in a shallow baking dish and pile the heated purée on top of each one. Be sure purée is not too thin.

3. Place the hot purée of peas in a shallow baking dish and cover with Mousseline Sauce*, to which you have added bottled horseradish to taste. Brown under broiler just before serving.

4. On a fried tomato slice.

5. Over a head of cooked cauliflower, thinning purée with cream so it will coat the cauliflower.

6. On large sautéed mushrooms. Good around steak.

CORN CUSTARD WITH FRIED TOMATOES

1 cup scraped corn
4 eggs, beaten
1 tablespoon minced onion
½ teaspoon salt
Dash of cayenne pepper or
    Tabasco sauce

1½ cups milk
3 medium tomatoes
2 tablespoons butter
Salt and pepper to taste
Chopped parsley

Preheat oven to 325° F. Combine the scraped corn (remove kernels with corn scraper or sharp knife), beaten eggs, minced onion, salt, and cayenne pepper or Tabasco (curry powder can be added for a different flavor). Scald milk and add it gradually. Pour into a shallow buttered casserole and place dish in a shallow pan of water. Bake for 30 minutes, or until custard is set.

Cut each tomato into 3 thick slices, fry in the butter, and season with salt and pepper. When tomatoes and custard are done, place slices of tomato on top of custard and sprinkle chopped parsley around each slice of tomato.

SERVES 6

CHERRY TOMATOES

Allow 4 to 6 per person. They should be of uniform size and firm. Scald very quickly and peel. This can be done ahead of time, even the morning of the party.

CAUTION: Do not put all of them in the water at once, as some will get soft and mushy. Keep them firm!

Five minutes before serving, heat the largest frying pan you have, add 4 tablespoons butter, 1 teaspoon Spice Islands Beau Monde seasoning, lots of chopped fresh chives and chopped parsley (basil optional), and mix all together. Drop peeled tomatoes (quickly) into the pan, place cover on top, and shake just long enough to heat them through. Do not overcook or they become mushy. Serve at once on a hot platter garnished with chives and parsley.

These are good with beef, in a spinach ring, or to decorate a fish platter.

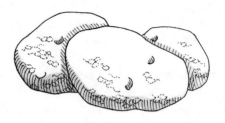

POMMES ANNA

The trick to these potatoes is that they are raw, sautéed in clarified butter in a black iron skillet.

Peel potatoes and slice about ¼ inch thick, and cover with cold water until ready to cook. Pour off all water, dry thoroughly on a towel, and sprinkle well with salt and plenty of freshly ground pepper. Place 2 tablespoons or more clarified butter in a black iron skillet to cover bottom of pan well; then lay the sliced potatoes around outside edge, working inward. Pour a little more clarified butter over top and place another lapping layer (never use more than 3 layers), then more butter.

Turn heat on high until potatoes are brown underneath, carefully watching. Turn heat down, cover with a lid for 5 minutes, using a weight on top of cover. Remove lid and continue browning on low heat until potatoes are done. Run a knife around and push a spatula a little under edges. Place a round platter over pan and flip potatoes over onto it. They should turn out crusty on top and soft underneath.

CREAMED BAKED POTATOES

Idaho potatoes baked the day before, cooled, and refrigerated overnight make the best-flavored creamed potatoes. The next day make a thin cream sauce, chop the cold baked potatoes finely, and stir in sauce. Add plenty of butter and salt and ground black pepper to taste. Heat and serve.

Here is another unusual way to serve them. Cut cold baked potatoes in half lengthwise, scoop out centers (using grapefruit knife and teaspoon, being careful not to cut skins), chop finely, and mix in cream sauce as above. Place potato shells on cookie sheet, butter edges, and place in hot oven for 15 minutes until crisp on edges. Fill shells with warm creamed potatoes, place a pat of butter on top of each, and run under the broiler until hot and golden (about 5 minutes with the shells on cookie sheet near the bottom of the broiler). Grated cheese may also be sprinkled on top, which makes them look like traditional stuffed potatoes.

These creamed potatoes freeze well. Should you wish to make crisp potato skins for cocktails, proceed as follows:

Crisp Potato Skins for Hors d'Oeuvre

Preheat oven to 375°–400° F. Hollow out baked potato skins, using inside for creamed or sautéed potatoes, then cut the skins into long strips. Butter thoroughly, sprinkle with salt and ground pepper, and place in oven until crisp. These may be served with sour cream and chive dip, or without, and are delicious with cocktails. Also good with caviar and sour cream or a small spoonful of Dried Beef in Cream*.

CREAMED POTATOES AU BON GOÛT

(No flour added)

Peel raw potatoes and cut them in small cubes. Put cubes in a saucepan and add light cream (or half milk and half heavy cream) to just cover the potatoes. Add plenty of salt and ground black pepper and cook, stirring constantly with a wooden spoon, until potatoes are soft. Never let the liquid boil. When done, add a lump of butter and sprinkle with chopped chives and parsley.

These potatoes may be reheated the next day or made into potato cakes.

HASHED BROWN POTATOES

Proceed as for Pommes Anna*, only chop raw potatoes into small cubes. After placing clarified butter in iron skillet, put in potatoes, never deeper than 2 inches. Grated onion may be added to raw potatoes if desired. The only difference between the two recipes is the shape of the potatoes.

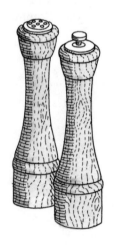

QUICK INSTANT-POTATO SOUFFLÉ

(For 6 small fish bakers, or 1 low baking dish, for luncheon)

1 cup milk, plus 2
   tablespoons
¼ cup mashed potatoes
   (packaged instant)
½ teaspoon salt
Pepper to taste
1 tablespoon butter

2 tablespoons chopped
   parsley
½ teaspoon Spice Islands
   fines herbes
2 egg yolks
4 egg whites

Heat milk just to boiling point. Stir in with wire whisk the potatoes, salt, pepper, butter, and herbs. Beat egg yolks and gradually add the hot potato mixture to the yolks. Cool slightly, then fold in egg whites, which you have beaten in a metal bowl until they form peaks.

SERVES 4 TO 6

Four Ways to Serve It

1. Combine crab meat or any cooked fish with a clam juice Béchamel (cream sauce with clam juice to taste). Place in small fish baker or shallow dish. Cover with potato soufflé and bake in preheated 400° F. oven for 10 to 12 minutes.

2. One cup of any cooked fish can be stirred into this soufflé mixture for a fish soufflé.

3. One cup grated sharp cheese, 1 tablespoon Worcestershire sauce, and ¼ teaspoon Dijon mustard added to the soufflé makes a delicious and easy cheese soufflé.

4. Place cooked flaked fish in shallow baking dish, cover with potato soufflé mixture, bake in quick 450° F. oven for about 15 minutes, and surround outer edge with Mousseline Sauce for fish* (number 6 of the Variations for Hollandaise*).

For larger soufflé, double above recipes.

CURRIED RICE

¾ stick (6 tablespoons)
   butter
1 cup unwashed long-grain
   rice

2 (10½-ounce) cans
   Campbell's beef consommé
1 teaspoon curry powder

In a frying pan, melt the butter. Add the rice and cook, stirring, until rice is golden and butter bubbles. Add the consommé and curry, cover, and simmer for exactly 40 minutes.

This is delicious circling chicken hash, creamed turkey, or pounded lamb chops. If you wish the rice drier, uncover pan and put it in a moderate oven (350° F.) for 15 to 20 minutes; however, it is much the best when moist.

Serves 4, or makes a border for a dish serving 6.

If you have any left over, or wish to do it all this way, place cooked rice in Cuisinart with a little cream and process. Use as a border for fish or meat.

SERVES 4

FLUFFY RICE

Cook 1½ cups long-grain rice in plenty of boiling water with juice of 1 lemon. When tender, in about 15 minutes, drain and run hot water over rice in colander. Fluff with a fork and keep warm by placing colander over a pan filled with simmering water. If you want it very dry, pour rice on a cookie sheet, place in 200° F. oven, and tease with a fork from time to time until dry.

If desired, butter may be added to the hot rice before serving.

SERVES 6

HERBED RICE

1 medium onion, finely
  chopped
¾ stick (6 tablespoons)
  butter
1 cup unwashed long-grain
  rice

2⅔ cups chicken stock
  (preferably homemade)
1 teaspoon Spice Islands fines
  herbes
1 cup chopped parsley

In a frying pan, sauté the onion in the butter until onion is golden. Add the rice and cook, stirring, until rice is golden (never brown). Add the chicken stock, herbs, and three quarters of the parsley. Cover and simmer for 40 minutes, or until all the stock is absorbed. Before serving, sprinkle remaining parsley on top.

This is good with chicken, veal, and fish.

SERVES 4

TARRAGON RICE

6 shallots, finely chopped
¾ stick (6 tablespoons)
  butter
1 cup unwashed long-grain
  rice

2⅔ cups chicken stock
3 tablespoons fresh tarragon
  or 1½ tablespoons dried
1 cup chopped parsley

In a frying pan, sauté the shallots in the butter until golden. Add the rice and cook, stirring, until the rice is golden (never brown). Add the chicken stock, tarragon, and three quarters of the parsley. Cover and simmer for about 40 minutes, until the stock is absorbed. Before serving, sprinkle remaining parsley on top.

This is very good served around edge of chicken, veal, or fish, or with a cooked seafood mixed to make a risotto.

SERVES 4 TO 6

VIVI'S RICE

(There is never any left!)

⅓ cup long-grain rice
1 cup heavy cream
1 pat butter
Salt and pepper to taste
1 small onion, chopped and
  sautéed

1 (16-ounce) can tomatoes
  (or the equivalent of
  peeled and seeded fresh
  tomatoes)
Fresh or dried basil to taste

Place all ingredients in a double boiler, cover, and simmer 1½ hours. Stir just before you serve it in a heated serving dish, or use as a border around any meat.

I have found you can add leftover pieces of chicken, ham, or fish, and serve in a casserole.

SERVES 4

SPINACH SOUFFLÉ SURPRISE

Make 4 poached eggs (the French way, in vinegar water so the white coats the yolk).* As soon as possible (eggs must be very soft), remove from water with skimmer. Trim edges and place in bowl of water. Place in refrigerator for 4 hours—they must be very cold.

Wash 1 pound spinach leaves, remove all stems, and cook briefly, as in the following basic Spinach* recipe. Place in Cuisinart and process with 1 onion or 2 shallots, peeled, plus ½ pear, until blended.

Cook a roux with 3 rounded tablespoons each of butter and all-purpose flour. When thick, add 1¼ cups milk. Cook again until it makes a thick sauce, adding salt and pepper to taste, pinch of nutmeg, and the processed spinach. Remove from stove and beat in 4 slightly beaten egg yolks. Set aside to really cool. (May be done ahead.)

Beat 6 egg whites, until stiff, with a pinch of salt. Take one quarter of egg whites and beat quickly into sauce. Fold in remaining whites with wooden paddle, using up and down movement, allowing air to get into mixture. Don't worry if all whites are not completely mixed.

Preheat oven to 375° F. Put half of mixture in an unbuttered 1½-quart soufflé dish. Remove eggs from refrigerator, drain on paper towel, and place on top of soufflé. Cover with remaining soufflé mixture. Sprinkle grated cheese the size of the poached eggs on top of each so you know where eggs are hidden (cheese will make a brown oval). Bake 25 minutes.

These poached eggs are not easy to make. They may be replaced with a layer of sliced hard-boiled eggs.

Hollandaise Sauce* is good served with this.

SERVES 4

* I use the French egg poachers, oval tins with holes in them and wire handles, which you place in simmering water just to cover, adding 2 tablespoons of vinegar and 1 teaspoon salt to water, as swirling the water in the true French way is complicated for most people!

SPINACH

Wash well 3 pounds spinach and remove all stems, even the stem in the middle of the leaf. Place wet spinach in a large kettle. Cook and stir over high heat. When just barely wilted, run cold water over spinach in a sieve and then squeeze water out with hands.

Process in Cuisinart with ½ fresh or canned pear. If canned, wash off sweet juice in a sieve with cold water before using. Reheat spinach before serving, adding lots of butter if your diet permits.

Try adding a drop of Pernod to the spinach for an interesting flavor.

SERVES 6

YELLOW SQUASH AU BON GOÛT

Allow 2 halves per person. Cut small yellow crookneck squash in half and steam or boil until almost cooked (do not let them get too soft). Remove inside of squash and fill with Purée of Peas*. Cover with buttered bread crumbs, sprinkle with Parmesan cheese, and bake until hot, running under broiler if not brown enough. These can be prepared ahead of time and then heated and browned. You can also fill squash with creamed mushrooms, cut-up tomatoes, or creamed peas and carrots. Always sprinkle filling with dots of butter, bread crumbs, and cheese.

SOUFFLÉS IN TOMATO SHELLS

6 large tomatoes
4 whole cloves
3 teaspoons grated onion
2 to 3 leaves basil
2 tablespoons butter
2 tablespoons all-purpose
  flour

¾ cup hot milk or light
  cream
3 eggs, separated
Salt and pepper to taste
1 teaspoon cognac

1. *Tomato Soufflé*. Cut a 1-inch slice from the tops of the 6 tomatoes and scoop out the pulp. Save the pulp and set the tomato shells to drain, saving any further juice also. Simmer the pulp and the juice, with the cloves, grated onion, and basil, until reduced to slightly more than 1 cup. Put through a strainer, mashing so that you get everything but the seeds.

In a saucepan, melt the butter and stir in the flour. When smooth, add the hot milk or cream. Cook and stir until thick and smooth.

Beat the egg yolks until light in color. Put a little of the hot cream sauce into the egg yolks, then a little more, and then the lot, stirring briskly between additions. Add the tomato purée, season to taste with salt and pepper, and add the cognac. Cool. Beat the egg whites until stiff but not dry. Stir a quarter of the whites into the sauce and then pour the sauce over the rest of the whites, folding in lightly.

Preheat the oven to 375° F. Cut a very thin slice from the bottom of each tomato so that it may stand upright in the pan. Fill tomatoes three-quarters full, place them in a shallow baking pan, and bake for 25 to 30 minutes. Surround with Mornay Sauce*, seasoned with a little Worcestershire.

2. *Cheese Soufflé** in tomato shells, prepared as described above.

3. Fish, spinach, or mushrooms can also be used in the soufflé and served with a Béchamel Sauce*. If using mushrooms, season sauce with 1 teaspoon allspice for an interesting flavor.
SERVES 6

SUGGESTION FOR LUNCHEON: Cold soup, any of these soufflés, green salad, and fruit dessert.

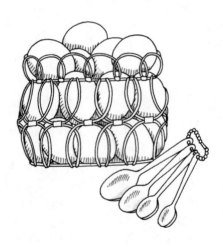

ZUCCHINI AU BON GOÛT

Prepare zucchini as in Zucchini Margo*. Fill cavities with chopped peeled fresh tomatoes mixed with small buttered croutons, salt, and freshly ground pepper. Cover with grated Cheddar or Parmesan cheese and bake in a preheated 450° F. oven just long enough to heat through. Just before serving, place zucchini under broiler to brown.

SERVES 6

ZUCCHINI FANS

6 very small zucchini
Melted butter
4 to 6 shallots, peeled and
    finely chopped
Reduced tomato sauce
    (made of fresh or canned
    tomatoes, onions, tomato
    paste, and basil)*

Grated Parmesan cheese
Paprika

Preheat oven to 325° F. Wash but do not peel the zucchini. Slice lengthwise, making 3 cuts, but do not cut through base, so you may spread each zucchini out like a fan. Butter a cookie sheet well, space fans on it, and sprinkle generously with melted butter and finely chopped shallots. Bake in oven. Halfway through cooking (after about 10 minutes), press down on each zucchini with a spatula to spread it out a little more. Remove from oven when done but still crisp. Spread tomato sauce within each fan opening and sprinkle with Parmesan cheese and paprika. Brown under broiler for a few minutes.

SERVES 4, GIVING 2 EXTRA

* Make at least 1 cup sauce, freezing any not used.

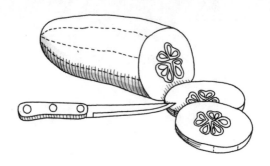

ZUCCHINI MARGO

9 small or 6 large zucchini
Salt
6 to 9 shallots or small
   onions, peeled and
   chopped

1 cup sour cream
1 cup grated Cheddar and
   Parmesan cheese mixed

Simmer or steam zucchini for 10 to 15 minutes, or until just tender. Do not overcook. Drain and, when cool, cut in half lengthwise and scoop out the seeds. Invert on paper towels to drain. Arrange zucchini, open side up, in a shallow baking pan. Salt lightly. Fill cavities first with chopped sautéed shallots or onions, then with sour cream, and sprinkle the cheese generously on top. Broil until cheese browns.

These can be prepared ahead of time, then heated in the oven before broiling.

SERVES 6

ZUCCHINI MOUSSELINE

Prepare zucchini as in Zucchini Margo (see preceding recipe). Fill cavities with Mousseline Sauce* and run under the broiler until golden brown.

SERVES 6

Meats
and Poultry

DRIED BEEF IN CREAM

If you can find a butcher who has a large piece of dried beef, which he will slice paper-thin, you will find it far the best and it is not necessary to rinse away salt. If not, buy the packaged dried beef, taste, and if it's salty, rinse with cold water in a sieve. Tear into small pieces and dry between paper towels. Sauté in clarified butter, sprinkling with 2 tablespoons all-purpose flour. When brown and crisp, add cream, milk, or half-and-half, or a combination of them, totaling about 2 cups. Stir until thickened. Season with Worcestershire sauce to taste.

2½ OUNCES SERVE 4

Following are two ways to change the flavor:

1. Add fresh or bottled horseradish to your taste.

2. Add a few drops of Hickory Liquid Smoke.

Both are delicious. Any of these can be served with the usual baked potato or toast points.

FOOLPROOF RARE ROAST BEEF

Sprinkle salt and pepper on a beef roast—2, 3, or 4 ribs. Place in preheated 375° F. oven for exactly 1 hour. Then turn off oven but never open the oven door.

It is important that the beef stand, after roasting, for at least 2 hours. Minutes before serving time, turn the oven on again to 300° F. and reheat 2 ribs for 14 to 15 minutes, 3 ribs 18 to 20 minutes, and 4 ribs 26 to 28 minutes.

It will be rare and perfect, with juices all the way through, and ready to carve immediately. But remember, the oven door is never opened from the beginning of cooking to the completion!

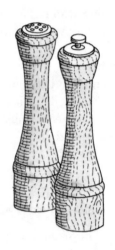

HAMBURGER

Everyone has a favorite way of making a hamburger, and this is mine.

1 onion
Clarified butter to cover pan
1 pound lean top round of
  beef
4 marrows from the bone,
  blanched 1 minute

Salt and pepper to taste
Worcestershire or Kikkoman
  soy sauce to taste

Chop onion finely in Cuisinart, sauté in clarified butter, and return to Cuisinart with chunks of round, marrows, and seasonings, being careful not to overprocess.
SERVES 4

Hamburger Hints

1. Never press or mold too firmly; rather, use hands to form lightly.

2. Half a cube of ice placed in the center of a hamburger gives it moisture and keeps it very rare.

3. Adding a beaten egg to a pound of ground round also makes a good moist hamburger.

HAMBURGER TURNOVERS HEALY

Take your favorite hamburger recipe and, to a scant ¼ pound, add 1 teaspoon fine dried bread crumbs. Place between wax paper and pound paper-thin with wooden tenderizer, such as is used for cubed steak. It may break through paper, but paper pulls off easily and leaves you with a 6-inch round with holes all over it. (If you do not have a tenderizer, use an end of a teaspoon and make holes all over.)

Remove wax paper from top and have an iron skillet piping hot with a little clarified butter in it (enough to cover bottom of pan). Flip round into skillet and brown only a few seconds *on one side only.* Add any desired filling and fold over like an omelet. It is very rare inside and can be served for a special dinner. with any of the following:

Fillings

1. Reduced tomatoes with crisp buttered croutons.

2. Creamed mushrooms.

3. Peeled and seeded tomatoes, cut into small squares and mixed with Béarnaise Sauce*.

4. Any filling of your own.

POUNDED BEEF

1. Ask your butcher to cut a filet mignon into slices a little over ¼ inch thick. Take these slices, put them between wax paper, and pound with the flat side of a cleaver until meat is paper-thin (even thinner than veal scallopini). Make a Bordelaise Sauce*. When it is bubbling, place the filets in the sauce for about 1 minute. Turn them and cook for about ½ minute longer. They must be pink inside.

2. Cut minute steaks as thin as a slice of roast beef, removing any bone. Pound the meat in the above fashion. Sauté the slices quickly in butter and serve with Bordelaise Sauce* or Béarnaise Sauce* or with just a little sauce made in the pan with flour, glace de viande, Worcestershire sauce, and water. Sprinkle with chopped parsley.

3. You can also cut slices from an uncooked roast of beef and treat them in the same way.

4. Pound a ½-inch slice of filet as thin as a scallopini. Sauté quickly in clarified butter on 1 side only. Have some creamed mushrooms ready in a double boiler. Place mushrooms in center of uncooked side of beef and fold over like an omelet. A Decorated Mushroom* looks well on top. The filet may also be filled with a reduced purée of fresh or canned tomatoes seasoned with onions, bread crumbs, and herbs of your choice. This is an inexpensive and easy way to serve a filet and also impressive.

5. Proceed as in Number 4, but instead of a filling of mushrooms or tomatoes, cut a round of dried white bread the size of the filet, then cut it in half and sauté in clarified butter until crisp. Fold filet over one half of sautéed bread. Place Béarnaise Sauce* around edges and sprinkle with chopped parsley or watercress leaves.

Always surround edges of folded beef with chopped parsley or watercress.

When sautéing several filets, they can be done on a grill rather than in an iron skillet.

I serve Number 5 for what I consider a different and delicious entrée that is not expensive!

CHICKEN AU BON GOÛT

This recipe, in the old days, took 3 hours or more to prepare. Now, with the Cuisinart, using the knife blade, it can be done in 3 minutes!

6 chicken breasts
¼ pound round steak
2 slices white bread
2½ teaspoons salt
1¾ cups heavy cream
1 tablespoon freshly ground pepper

1 medium onion or 6 to 8 shallots
2 eggs
2 teaspoons dried tarragon or 1 full tablespoon fresh tarragon (optional)

Remove skins from boned chicken breasts. Cut chicken and round steak into 1-inch pieces. Place in Cuisinart work bowl with the remaining ingredients. Process until smooth and creamy.

Melt 3 tablespoons butter or (preferably) clarified butter in an iron skillet and drop chicken mixture by spoonfuls to form a cake, small or large, as you wish. Cook at one time as many as you can get into pan without crowding. Brown on one side, turn, reduce heat, and cook for 5 minutes.

Raw or cooked, the mixture freezes well. Your leftover cakes, sliced, make delicious sandwiches or are good served cold as a meat dish.

My favorite way of serving Chicken Au Bon Goût is with a Tarragon Butter Rose on top of each patty, which is rich in itself; however, I have included variations and sauces.

SERVES 6 TO 8

Tarragon Butter Rose

Bring 1 stick of butter to room temperature. Mix in fresh or dried tarragon to your taste, adding a squeeze of lemon juice.

Form back into a stick, rewrap in its paper, and freeze, or refrigerate until firm.

When ready to use, remove from freezer and bring to room temperature. Slice into 6 or 8 pieces. Take a 4-prong fork and roll each corner of butter upward to form the petals of the roses. I also make these roses, without tarragon, to place on bread and butter plates when serving bread.

VARIATIONS

Following are three different combinations of meats, and sauces that can be served with them, all done the same way as Chicken Au Bon Goût.

Round Steak: Take 2½ pounds round steak, cut into 1-inch squares, and proceed as in recipe.

Veal: Take 2 pounds veal plus ½ pound round steak, or use all veal, cut into 1-inch squares, then proceed as in recipe.

Lamb: Bone 6 shoulder lamb chops and remove all fat and gristle, or use 2½ pounds leg of lamb cut into 1-inch squares. Proceed as for chicken, except use 3 cloves garlic instead of the onion.

Sauces for These Variations

1. Chop parsley with knife in work bowl of Cuisinart, then stir into melted butter. Add capers to taste.

2. Madeira.

3. Slice mushrooms with slicer and add to a cream sauce. (I use a hard-boiled egg slicer.)

4. Tarragon or parsley butter.

5. Soubise Sauce*.

CHICKEN BREASTS MANY WAYS

To prepare, skin breasts and, using a very sharp knife, remove bones (or buy them boned, which costs more!). You still have to remove the sinew by taking one end with a paper towel and sliding knife along it to finally pull it out. Taking care to unfold fillet and lay it flat by the side of the breast, pound chicken very thin between wax paper. Sprinkle with salt, pepper, and a squeeze of lemon. Sauté quickly in clarified butter, about 3 minutes to a side. Remove to a platter and serve with any of the following sauces, Numbers 1–5. (You may also cook chicken breasts in clarified butter in a covered casserole, time about the same.)

1. Cover breasts with a sauce made as for fricassee, adding lots of chopped, fresh tarragon (only half as much if using dried) to a strong homemade chicken stock thickened with beurre manié.* The French way is to thicken with egg yolks, but the sauce curdles easily, especially if it has to wait. Serve in a shallow casserole with pastry cutouts standing up all around; see chicken pattern in Cuisinart Piecrust* recipe.

2. A mushroom sauce made with a rich Béchamel* with dry vermouth added.

3. Place on sautéed toast and spread with chopped cooked chicken livers. Make sauce as follows: to a rich Béchamel Sauce* add bottled or freshly grated horseradish and sherry to your taste. If using fresh horseradish, strain before serving. Pour sauce over the chicken. This was a specialty aboard the *Île de France*.

4. Serve with Bordelaise Sauce* and top with a Decorated Mushroom*.

Beurre manié: Blend equal parts of flour and butter together and keep in refrigerator or freezer; it helps you thicken sauces quickly without lumps.

---

5. Place on sautéed toast and spread with chopped cooked chicken livers, not overcooked. Make a pan sauce using a little flour, chicken stock, glace de viande, and a little white wine. Cover breast with sauce, top with broiled Decorated Mushroom*, and surround with watercress.

6. Squeeze lemon over raw chicken breasts and season with salt and pepper. Dip breasts in beaten egg and then in *coarse* fresh bread crumbs. Drop in deep, hot clarified butter as if you were using vegetable shortening. Cooking time: 4 or 5 minutes. (This clarified butter may be strained and used many times for deep frying.) Test for correct heat by dropping a piece of bread in butter; if it browns at once, butter is at right temperature. The fried chicken breasts may be served with sauces 1, 2, or 4.

7. Rub with garlic, squeeze lemon juice over, and marinate for at least ½ hour. Brown breasts in clarified butter, place in a casserole, shake Kikkoman soy sauce, to taste, over them, and bake in a hot oven for 30 minutes. You can also serve half broilers this way.

8. If you have leftover cooked turkey or chicken, place slices on a sautéed piece of toast and cover with Mousseline Sauce*. Run under broiler to heat and brown. Quick and delicious.

CHICKEN HASH RITZ CARLTON

This is a hash we all of a certain age remember; here is my version.

7 chicken breasts	1 cup heavy cream
2 cups chicken stock, homemade or canned	1 scant cup chicken stock
	3 egg yolks
3½ tablespoons butter	1 tablespoon lemon juice
5 tablespoons all-purpose flour	⅔ stick (5⅓ tablespoons) butter
1 cup light cream	½ cup cream, whipped

Poach skinned and boned chicken breasts in chicken stock to cover for 10 minutes, or until firm to the touch. Remove chicken breasts and, when cool, cut into long thin strips and then into tiny neat squares. Reserve the stock.

Make a roux of the 3½ tablespoons butter and the flour, adding the light cream and, when the sauce thickens, the heavy cream plus 1 scant cup of the reserved chicken stock (the sauce should not be too thin). Stir in the chicken squares and allow it to sit for an hour or more. Sometimes I leave it in the refrigerator covered overnight, as the chicken absorbs some of the cream.

You may serve this hash with mashed potatoes, piped around the edge with a pastry tube or simply spooned around, or with Purée of Peas*, to which you can add ½ cup of mashed potatoes, as you prefer.

When ready to serve, preheat oven to 350° F. Place the creamed chicken in a low baking dish and make a Mousseline sauce of the egg yolks, lemon juice, and ⅔ stick butter, following the Hollandaise Sauce* recipe and adding ½ cup whipped cream to the Hollandaise.

Spread this over the top of hash and place in oven for 10 to 15 minutes. If not brown enough, place under broiler at the end for a few seconds.

Pipe the Purée of Peas or mashed potatoes around the edge and serve. I prefer the Purée of Peas as a border because of the color and taste.

If you have leftover turkey or roast chicken, you may prepare it the same way. Leaving the meat in the sauce for several hours makes it more moist and tastier.

SERVES 4 OR 5

CHICKEN LUCY

If you want a wonderfully rich chicken, soak 4 skinned and boned breasts in ½ pint light cream overnight. Strain. Place 1 tablespoon clarified butter in iron skillet and sauté breasts on both sides, being careful not to let them burn, for about 7 or 8 minutes. Salt and pepper if desired.

Serve with wild rice and currant jelly.

The strained cream may be frozen for future use in preparing this recipe or making a cream sauce for chicken. To use, proceed as in Whipped Cream* suggestion.

SERVES 4

CHICKEN IN SARAN THREE WAYS

4 *small* chicken breasts

Skin and bone the breasts and pound between wax paper until paper-thin.

Filling Number I: Curried Rice

Curried Rice*   Mango Sauce*
Saran wrap (4 pieces, 10   Chopped parsley
   inches long)   Major Grey's chutney

Make Curried Rice and place 2 good tablespoons in center of each chicken breast. Roll up and place in buttered center of Saran wrap. Roll Saran completely around chicken, overlapping it. Twist each end, one to the right, the other to the left, and tie a *tight* knot at each end of roll as close to chicken as possible. Place the 4 rolls in simmering water for 8 to 10 minutes. Remove with a slotted spoon onto paper towels, cut the knots, and take off the Saran wrap. Place chicken on a hot platter, cover with Mango Sauce, sprinkle with chopped parsley, and serve with Major Grey's chutney.

You may pile extra rice in center of platter, if you wish; otherwise, make only ½ recipe Curried Rice.

These rolls freeze well, as does the Curried Rice, so I usually make more than I wish to serve.

SERVES 4

Filling Number II: Creamed Mushrooms

½ pound mushrooms
4 shallots
1½ tablespoons clarified
  butter
1 scant tablespoon
  all-purpose flour

⅓ cup heavy cream
1 tablespoon dry vermouth
Béchamel Sauce*

Chop the mushrooms in Cuisinart with the shallots, using on-and-off method so they will not be too fine. Sauté in a pan with the clarified butter until juice disappears. Sprinkle on a scant tablespoon of flour, add the heavy cream and dry vermouth, and stir until thick.

Proceed with chicken rolls as in Number I, but fill with the creamed mushrooms.

These rolls may be sauced with a plain Béchamel or a Béchamel to which you have added a little wine or chicken stock to taste and sautéed sliced mushrooms.

SERVES 4

Filling Number III: Cold Chicken Au Bon Goût

½ recipe Chicken Au Bon
  Goût*

Spread with Chicken Au Bon Goût, roll, and proceed as in Number I. When rolls are cold, slice diagonally and serve for a buffet dish or with a green salad.

These rolls freeze well, as does the Chicken Au Bon Goût.

SERVES 4

CHICKEN PIE AU BON GOÛT

In the old days, stewing chickens made the best chicken pie. Today they are hard to find and, if found, they are frozen and sometimes have been for far too long, so here is my recipe made with two roasting chickens.

2 roasting chickens, cut into pieces
½ cup celery leaves
1 large onion stuck with a few cloves
6 sprigs parsley
Bouquet garni (herbs and peppercorns)
Water to just cover chicken in pot
1 Knorr-Swiss chicken cube
6 or 7 chicken wings
5 tablespoons chicken fat
6 tablespoons all-purpose flour
5½ to 6 cups chicken stock
1 drop yellow food coloring (optional)
Cuisinart Piecrust*
Bunch of parsley

Simmer first 8 ingredients 20 to 25 minutes, then remove white meat. Leave the dark meat simmering for about 40 to 45 minutes more. Remove all of the dark meat and reduce stock with wings for another 30 minutes. Strain through a fine sieve and place in refrigerator until fat comes to the top and you can remove it. Make a roux with 5 tablespoons of the chicken fat and the 6 tablespoons flour, adding the 5½ to 6 cups chicken stock. Add 1 drop yellow food coloring, which makes it look more like that stewing chicken you could not buy!

Remove skin and bones from pieces of chicken (I use only the breasts cut in half, thighs, and legs). Place in a round baking dish or Pyrex casserole and pour over the chicken gravy.

Make Cuisinart Piecrust and roll 1 inch larger all around than top of your dish, crimping edges. Cut 4 slits in pastry to hold chickens which you cut out of pastry with a chicken-shaped cutter. Bake crust and pastry chickens.

Place crust on top of chicken, which has been heated in the oven. Put the 4 chicken pastries in the slits, standing up. Place a bunch of parsley in center, as if chickens were eating some.

If guests are late, chicken and gravy are kept hot and crust is placed on top at last minute. Also, this way, gravy can be corrected if it is too thick or has cooked away, by adding more chicken stock or cream.

SERVES 6

I usually cook the chicken the previous day, add enough chicken stock to chicken pieces to keep them moist, and refrigerate chicken and stock overnight. The following day remove fat from stock, make the roux, and proceed with the recipe.

CHICKEN SARA

Skin and pound 4 boned chicken breasts until quite thin. Marinate in the juice of 1 lemon for 30 minutes. Sauté in clarified butter, about 2 or 3 minutes on each side. Reserve chicken on another dish; reserve butter and pan juices in pan.

Sauce

½ cup dry vermouth
½ cup dry white wine
½ cup peeled and chopped
    shallots
2 cups *strong* chicken stock

2 cups heavy cream
1 ounce morels (dried
    mushrooms), soaked in
    water for at least 30
    minutes

Boil the vermouth, white wine, shallots, and stock until reduced to ½ cup. Strain, add heavy cream, and reduce until thick.

Remove the mushrooms from water, chop, and sauté in the pan juices and butter left in the pan in which you sautéed the chicken. Add mushrooms to sauce and strain any remaining juices also into sauce. This may be made hours ahead, or even the previous day, as it improves with keeping.

When ready to serve breasts, spread lightly with Grey Poupon Dijon mustard, sprinkle with a few moist green peppercorns, and top with fine buttered bread crumbs. Run under broiler until hot and lightly browned. (Place pan halfway from flame in broiler and watch carefully!)

Heat sauce and pour onto a hot platter, place chicken breasts on top, and garnish with watercress.

SERVES 4

COLD CURRY CHICKEN SOUFFLÉ

1 envelope plus 1 teaspoon
   Knox unflavored gelatin
1½ (10¾-ounce) cans
   Campbell's cream of
   chicken soup
1¾ cups chicken stock
1½ to 2 tablespoons curry
   powder (to taste)

3 heaping cups cooked
   chicken, cut into small
   pieces, or 6 or 7 breasts,
   which you have poached
   in chicken stock
1 cup heavy cream, whipped
Mango or Major Grey's
   chutney

In a bowl, dissolve the gelatin in ¼ cup of the chicken stock. Heat the soup with the remaining 1½ cups chicken stock (instead of water, as directed on the label). Pour the gelatin in and bring to a boil, adding the curry powder. Return to bowl and stir until curry is dissolved. Add the chicken pieces. Refrigerate until it starts to jell, then fold in the whipped cream. Pour into a 1-quart soufflé dish, around which you have tied a buttered wax-paper collar. The soufflé, when jelled, should be a good inch above rim of dish. Refrigerate overnight or for at least 4 hours.

When ready to serve, remove paper collar and sprinkle sides and top with toasted sesame seeds, fine toasted bread crumbs, or even slivered toasted almonds. Serve with mango or Major Grey's chutney. This is good served with a cold vegetable salad, pita bread, and fruit for dessert.

This recipe, doubled, is excellent for a buffet.

SERVES 6

CHICKEN STRIPS WITH MANGO
SAUCE

With a sharp knife, bone 6 chicken breasts, or buy boned ones at your market (these cost more!). Remove skin, and also remove one large white tendon by holding the end with a paper towel and scraping against it with a knife, pulling tendon out. Remove fillet, cut with knife, then pound breast between wax paper once or twice. Cut breast into 3 long slices and trim the ends so all will be the same length. This will give you 4 slices, including the fillet.

Sprinkle flour, salt, and pepper on a large piece of wax paper and dredge the chicken strips, then remove excess flour by shaking them in a sieve.

Two or three minutes before you are ready to serve, sauté in clarified butter, first one side, then the other. When chicken is springy, it is done. These strips can be served with many different sauces. I usually serve them with the following Mango Sauce.
SERVES 6

Mango Sauce

(*With thanks to Polly*)

2½ cups heavy cream
3 tablespoons of mushroom
 ketchup (mushroom au
 jus, John Burger, London)
3 tablespoons Worcestershire
 sauce

3 tablespoons mango
 chutney, chopped into
 small pieces

Simmer all ingredients, to reduce cream and sauces, for about 6 minutes over medium heat. Pour over chicken strips and serve with rice. If you wish to make ahead, allow sauce to cool, pour over strips in a low baking dish, and reheat in 375° F. oven for 5 minutes, or until hot.

A thin Béchamel Sauce* may be substituted for the heavy cream.

PORK TENDERLOIN

An interesting way to serve pork tenderloin is to cut a slice about 1½ inches thick for each serving and pound between wax paper until paper-thin. Sauté on both sides in clarified butter in black iron skillet, approximately 5 minutes in all. Serve with fried tart apple rings, sprinkling them with a little brown sugar. Place on pork rounds and serve.

JINNIE'S PORK ROAST

Pork roast, 5 to 6 pounds
1 cup pitted dried prunes
3 cups peeled and cored
    apples
3 tablespoons heavy cream
Bourbon to taste
2 cups chicken stock

Marinade:
  ¼ cup bourbon
  ¼ cup Kikkoman soy
    sauce
  2 tablespoons Grey
    Poupon Dijon mustard
  ¼ cup chopped onions
  ¼ cup light brown sugar

Marinate roast overnight. Preheat oven to 350° F. Place roast, with the marinade, in a roasting pan in the oven. When half cooked (a little over an hour), remove and reserve all marinade and juices, and add the prunes and apples. Finish cooking. When done, remove roast to a platter, and place prunes on one side. The apples taste good but look messy, so I either discard them or purée them in the Cuisinart to add to the marinade plus 2 cups chicken stock before reducing it.

When roast is returned to the oven to finish cooking (a little over an hour), reduce marinade by half on top of stove. Remove all fat and strain. Add the heavy cream and some bourbon to taste. Pass with the roast.

SERVES 6 TO 8

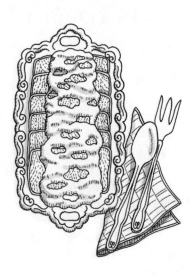

HAM BRADLEY

Sauté on both sides 6 thin slices cold boiled ham in a little clarified butter. Sprinkle with about 3 tablespoons brown sugar and sauté until a little caramelized, then add ¼ cup red wine vinegar and continue cooking for a minute or so. Remove from pan and place on shallow ovenproof serving dish or platter. Sprinkle each piece of ham with fine dry bread crumbs mixed with melted butter and with Grey Poupon Dijon mustard to taste. (This may be done ahead of time.) At the last moment, run under broiler until brown and crisp.

Ham is delicious served as a separate course with a green salad, gnocchi, sweetbreads, or creamed hard-boiled eggs.
SERVES 4

This recipe was made famous at Bradley's Gambling Club in Palm Beach years ago.

MYRTLE'S LEG OF LAMB

Myrtle, a wonderful black woman who was my cook and friend for eighteen years, learned this recipe from a Jamaican chef with whom she worked.

Take a leg of lamb weighing from 5½ to 7½ pounds. Ask the butcher to remove all fat. You may have to finish his job! Marinate it at least 8 hours, or overnight, in 1 bottle of the Christian Brothers dry white wine (my first choice) or any American dry white sauterne, adding 2 carrots and 2 medium onions cut in small pieces, 6 black peppercorns, 3 cloves, 2 bay leaves, and 1 teaspoon grated nutmeg.

Preheat oven to 350° F. Place leg of lamb in roasting pan and cook for 1½ hours. It should be pink. While lamb is roasting, put marinade in a pan on top of the stove and reduce to about half. Strain. Baste the lamb during last 10 minutes with about ¼ cup of the reduced marinade. Put lamb under the broiler for the last 5 minutes if not brown enough. Remove lamb to a heated platter. Strain pan juices, remove fat, and add juices to reduced marinade on stove, completing your sauce. If you wish it thicker, add 2 teaspoons potato starch diluted in ¼ cup cold water. The gravy should be thin and clear.

Cold Leftover Lamb

Slice lamb paper-thin and place overlapping on a platter. Make a sauce as follows: stir leftover gravy into 1 pint or more of sour cream. Cover lamb completely with sauce, then sprinkle with chopped parsley and capers.

I have been known to cook a leg of lamb the day before I wish to serve it cold with this sauce. It's so good, it need not be a leftover.

POUNDED LAMB MANY WAYS

Have your butcher (or you can do it yourself with a sharp knife) bone a double-rib lamb chop or a loin chop, taking off all fat and gristle. Pound the meat between two pieces of wax paper until it is about ½ inch thick (not as paper-thin as fillet of beef). Sauté in butter quickly (must be pink inside!) and serve in the following ways:

1. For a special dinner party, sauté slices of dried Pepperidge Farm bread in clarified butter quickly on both sides. Spread with pâté de foie gras and keep them warm on a platter. Place each sautéed pounded chop on top of a piece of bread and cover with a sauce made as follows:

Heat 1 (10-ounce) jar currant jelly to the boiling point and stir in 1 tablespoon potato starch mixed with ¼ cup cold water. Bring to a boil, stirring, and add dry sherry to taste. Garnish with watercress.

2. Place each sautéed chop on a piece of sautéed toast the size of the chop and put a large spoonful of Béarnaise Sauce* on top. (Try to have plenty of fresh tarragon in your sauce.) Sprinkle with chopped parsley.

3. Serve sautéed pounded lamb chops with a border of Curry Rice* and pass Major Grey's chutney. Sautéed toast may be put under each chop if desired.

4. Serve each sautéed pounded chop on a piece of sautéed toast. Cover with rich mushroom sauce, and garnish with parsley.

5. Poor Man's Lamb Chop: Pound chop. Place 2 tablespoons seasoned ground round steak at one side of the chop, making it the same height. Cook lightly a very thin strip of

bacon and wrap around the combined meats, securing with a toothpick. Sauté until either pink or well done, depending on your taste. You need not serve 2 chops per person!

6. Pound 1½-inch-thick boned rib chop between wax paper until paper-thin, giving you about a 4-inch round. Sauté in clarified butter in hot iron skillet on one side. Combine dried pieces of bread, softened butter, parsley, and Dijon mustard to taste in Cuisinart bowl, using knife blade, until finely blended. Spread uncooked side of chop with this mixture and run under hot broiler until golden brown. This is delicious served with Creamed Baked Potatoes* or Creamed Potatoes Au Bon Goût*, a green vegetable, and a light dessert.

CURRY OF LAMB MADRAS

1 cup minced carrots
1 cup minced onions
1 large clove garlic, minced

4 tablespoons clarified butter
1½ pounds lean lamb, cut
    into small chunks

Sauté the carrots, onions, and garlic in the clarified butter until well coated but not browned. Strain out the vegetables (discard or reserve for soup) and, in the same fat, brown the lean lamb (3 pounds shoulder yields about 1½ pounds after trimming). Remove all fat and cut into small chunks.

When browned, or at least well seared, add:

4 tablespoons all-purpose flour
6 tablespoons curry powder

Stir until flour is absorbed and meat browned, then add:

3 cups stock (2 Campbell's beef consommé
    and 1 chicken broth)
2 tablespoons tomato paste

Cook over very low heat until meat is almost tender, about 2½ hours, then add:

1 minced apple

½ cup raisins

Simmer for 5 minutes and, just before serving, add:

3 tablespoons heavy cream

Serve with Fluffy Rice* and the following:

1. Chopped peanuts
2. Fresh coconut, grated
3. Chutney
4. Chopped crisp-cooked bacon
5. Chopped hard-boiled eggs

SERVES 6

Lamb Curry Comment

The quality of the curry powder used is most important in this recipe.

My husband's response to this recipe was amusing. "This lamb curry should be served for lunch, never dinner. Utensils should be a dessert spoon and fork rather than a knife and fork. Also, beer is the only appropriate beverage to serve with it." This from a gentleman who lived in India.

CHARLOTTE'S LAMB MELON

(A quick version of other recipes)

Boned shoulder of lamb
Vegetable oil or clarified
  butter
2 large carrots, sliced
2 large onions, sliced
1 can beef consommé
1 cup dry white wine or ½
  cup dry vermouth

1 can chicken stock or broth
  (homemade is best)
1 (10¼-ounce) can
  Franco-American beef
  gravy
Lamb bones (ask butcher to
  cut)

Combine the following to make the stuffing:

½ pound butter
4 cloves garlic, finely minced
8 to 10 shallots, finely minced
2 tablespoons each fresh
  chives, chervil, parsley (if
  dried, ½ teaspoon each)
1 teaspoon dried thyme

1 egg
9 or 10 slices dried or stale
  bread (thick and good
  bread), made into bread
  crumbs
Salt and freshly ground black
  pepper to taste

Stuff the lamb, shape it like a melon with the help of aluminum foil, and put into the freezer for 10 minutes. Remove foil and tie, retaining melon shape. Sear in vegetable oil or clarified butter.

Preheat oven to 450° F. Put lamb into a roasting pan on top of the carrots and onions. Add the consommé, wine, chicken stock, beef gravy, and bones.

Roast, uncovered, for 20 minutes at 450° F. Turn to 350° F. and cook, covered, until done (2½ to 3 hours). Baste every half hour.

One half hour before done, remove lamb from pan, take out bones, strain juices, and degrease. Return to oven and finish roasting. The vegetables may be puréed and used to thicken the sauce.

SERVES 6

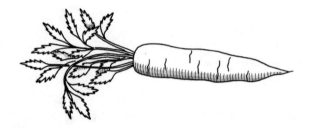

VEAL PORTOFINO

1 pound lean shoulder of
    veal, cut in pieces
2 slices Pepperidge Farm
    white bread, crumbled
1 medium onion, cut in
    pieces

2½ teaspoons salt
⅛ teaspoon pepper
1 egg
1 cup light cream

Place all ingredients in Cuisinart and process, using knife blade, until mixture is light and fluffy. Refrigerate for an hour or more until mixture stiffens. With wet hands, shape the meat into patties and sauté them quickly in hot clarified butter on both sides. Reduce heat and cook patties slowly for about 10 minutes, turning them twice, and serve with sauce Number 1 or Number 2.

1. A brown butter sauce to which is added 2 tablespoons capers, a little lemon juice or vinegar, and chopped parsley.

2. Melt 1 tablespoon of butter and add 1 heaping tablespoon of flour. Stir with wire whip until smooth, then add 1 cup chicken stock, 3 tablespoons glace de viande (optional), and 3 tablespoons Madeira. (This sauce can be doubled and frozen to have on hand.)

These patties can be made with creamed mushrooms between thin patties.
SERVES 6

For the diet-conscious, use 1 cup chicken stock instead of the cream, 1 slightly beaten egg white, ¼ cup chopped parsley mixed with 1 teaspoon tarragon, black pepper, and the juice of 1 small onion. Serve with one of the following sauces:

1. Serve with sauce made of margarine instead of butter.

2. Place a sprig of rosemary in pan in which you sauté the veal. Sprinkle with grated skim-milk mozzarella cheese and run under broiler for a minute, adding a little Madeira if desired.

VEAL MARTINE

Ask butcher for 6 thin veal birds or 6 scallopini. These are pounded between wax paper until paper-thin.

Pat flour, salt, and pepper on both sides of the veal. Shake off excess flour in strainer and sauté in black iron skillet. When slightly brown, place 6 slices prosciutto on top of the veal. Shake pan and cook a bit, then drop paper-thin slices of imported Swiss cheese on ham. Add 3 tablespoons Marsala or white wine, and salt and pepper to taste. Cover for a few minutes, add 2 tablespoons glace de viande (optional) and light cream to make enough sauce for each slice of veal.

SERVES 4

VEAL WITH SOUBISE SAUCE

Veal: Sauté quickly on both sides 4 paper-thin veal cutlets until tender (takes a few minutes), place in a shallow baking dish, and, with a wide pastry tube, pipe the sauce (see below) around the cutlets. Run under the broiler just before serving. (With the average veal available to most of us, I find it helps to marinate it in lemon juice for at least an hour.)

Soubise Sauce: Chop a *large* white Bermuda onion into very small pieces and cook (but do not brown it at all) in 3 tablespoons clarified butter. Add 1 cup precooked packaged rice (Uncle Ben's) and 1¼ cups well-flavored chicken broth. Bring to a boil and cook gently for about 5 minutes. Place in a blender or Cuisinart with 4 or 5 tablespoons fresh cooked mushrooms, a sprig of parsley, 1 egg yolk, and 4 tablespoons thick cream. Process until very smooth. Adjust the seasoning, adding salt and pepper if necessary. Keep warm in a double boiler.
SERVES 4

NOTE: Soubise may be served as a border for many things by piping sauce around the edge of the flat baking dish, with whatever meat you wish in the center, and running it under the broiler to brown at the last moment. The French reassemble a sliced rolled boned roast of veal by spreading Soubise between the slices.

VEAL ZINGARA

Sauce for Veal

¼ pound finely chopped mushrooms
Squeeze of lemon
4 thin slices cold boiled tongue or ham, cut in strips

Not quite a box of frozen artichoke hearts, each heart cut into about 4 slices, at room temperature
¼ cup Marsala

Sauté mushrooms in 2 tablespoons clarified butter for about 3 or 4 minutes, adding a squeeze of lemon. In another pan sauté ham or tongue strips in butter for a few minutes, then add mushrooms and sliced artichoke hearts. Cook until artichokes are done, adding about ¼ cup Marsala. This should make enough sauce to coat each slice of veal and not be runny.

Veal: Take 6 paper-thin pieces of veal, which have been pounded between wax paper. Put a little flour, seasoned with salt and pepper, on both sides, and sauté quickly in a little clarified butter, about 1½ minutes on each side.

Place veal on a heated platter and cover each piece with sauce, not allowing it to run off. Sprinkle with chopped parsley and serve at once. If you wish a richer sauce, use 4 tablespoons of Bordelaise Sauce* instead of the Marsala.

SERVES 6

NOTE: If your veal is not of the best quality, marinate for about an hour in lemon juice, dry, and proceed with recipe.

Fish

Fish

FLOUNDER OR SHRIMP QUENELLES

2 pounds raw flounder or 1½
    pounds large shelled and
    deveined shrimp
1½ cups heavy cream,
    adding a little more if
    needed

2 eggs
½ cup chopped parsley
Pinch of cayenne pepper
Salt and pepper to taste
½ teaspoon grated nutmeg

Place all ingredients in Cuisinart bowl and blend with the knife blade until smooth and creamy.

Mold egg-shaped quenelles by using 2 dessert spoons, dipping spoons in hot water after each quenelle is formed. Butter a shallow roasting pan and place over two burners. Put in the quenelles and gently pour boiling water in at the side of pan. Allow water to simmer, turning quenelles once. When they float and are springy to the touch, remove with a slotted spoon to paper towels.

Butter a shallow baking dish, arrange the quenelles in it, and pour over and around them Pink Fish Sauce*. Decorate with Parsley en Pluches*.

SERVES 6

FLOUNDER NORWAY

6 small fillets flounder

2 (8-ounce) bottles clam
juice, or fish stock, plus
water

Béchamel Sauce*

¾ cup chopped fresh dill

½ cup chopped parsley

4 finely chopped shallots

Dry vermouth

Pastry Fish

Poach the 6 small fillets flounder (or any delicate white fish) in the clam juice, adding water just to cover, for about 6 minutes, or until firm and white. Lift fillets out of pan with a slotted spatula and place in a shallow oblong dish with sides about 1½ inches high. Cover with a sauce made as follows:

Make Béchamel Sauce and, when hot, add ¼ cup of the strained clam juice in which fish was poached plus the fresh dill, parsley, and shallots. Reduce for about 5 minutes or more. Check consistency of sauce, adding a little vermouth or fish stock if needed. Pour over fillets, decorating dish all around the sides with Pastry Fish by placing head and tails in as if swimming.

SERVES 4

Pastry Fish

Make Cuisinart Piecrust*, doubling the recipe but making only one recipe at a time. Roll out, place cardboard or paper pattern on top, and cut around fish head and tails. It will take about 8 or 9 of each, depending on the size of dish. Bake as directed and keep them in a tightly covered tin, or freeze them if you make a few days ahead.

If you do not use pattern given (the drawing is the correct size for the pastry pattern), try to find a fish cookie cutter. When baked, stand fish around sides of dish.

QUICK FISH IN SHELLS

Place any cooked fish or seafood (crab meat is especially good) in small fish shells, as for Coquilles St. Jacques. Put the shells on a cookie sheet and, just before serving, cover fish in each ramekin (do not stir in) with 2½ tablespoons sauce, made as follows:

Combine mayonnaise with a dash of Tabasco, a squeeze of lemon, and enough ketchup to make the sauce pink. (You can substitute sour cream for the mayonnaise.) Run the shells under the broiler until they are a lovely pinky-brown on top.

If you wish to make this fish in large quantities in a baking dish, heat the fish first in a double boiler, then put in baking dish, cover fish with sauce, and run under the broiler.

CRAB MEAT IN CHAFING DISH

This is an old recipe from the College Inn in Chicago.

1 pound fresh crab meat,
lump style
1 stick (½ cup) butter
4 tablespoons tarragon
vinegar
2 tablespoons Lea & Perrins
Worcestershire sauce

Lots of freshly ground black
pepper and salt to taste
½ cup chopped chives
2 sprigs fresh tarragon leaves
or 1 tablespoon dried
tarragon
½ cup chopped parsley

Inspect the crab meat for any shells. Heat in a double boiler until just warm. Heat the butter in a chafing dish or pan until very hot but not brown, and add the vinegar, Worcestershire, salt, pepper, chives, tarragon, and parsley. Finally add the crab meat.

Serve in soup bowls if used for a main course. Great for luncheons. This was always served in a chafing dish, but it certainly is not necessary.

SERVES 6 FOR FIRST COURSE, 4 FOR MAIN COURSE

POTATO-SHRIMP MOLD

Take 2 cups cubed boiled potatoes (do not overcook) and marinate while still warm with ¼ cup My French Dressing*. Add 3 or 4 sliced hard-boiled eggs and some chopped onion to taste, stirring carefully. Season with salt and pepper to taste and cool.

Fold in mayonnaise as desired.

Decorate the inside of a round, buttered bowl with about 1 pound cooked medium shrimp. (The entire mold should be covered with shrimp.) Fill with salad mixture and pack down firmly. Chill for several hours.

Unmold and place a cooked pea in the center of each shrimp. Decorate with lettuce, watercress, and tomatoes around the mold.

SERVES 4 TO 6

NOTE: If you wish to cut down on the expense, split the shrimps in half. You have the same look with half the amount of shrimp!

This can be made in individual molds for a Nouvelle Cuisine salad: see Potato Salad and Sliced Beef*.

SHRIMPS GRAND VÉFOUR

4 slices of Pepperidge Farm
toasting white bread, or 4
thick slices cut from
unsliced bread, hollowed
out slightly with a sharp
knife

1 pound raw shrimp
2 teaspoons sea salt
16 peppercorns

Sauce:

1 cup dry white wine
2 teaspoons tomato purée
or paste
4 chopped shallots or
scallions
2 chopped carrots
2 chopped onions
4 tablespoons butter
4 tablespoons vegetable oil
1 cup water
Herb bouquet

2 tablespoons cognac, flamed
2 tablespoons heavy cream
2 tablespoons butter, in small
pieces
1 teaspoon cornstarch,
dissolved in 1 tablespoon
cold water
6 tablespoons butter
2 tablespoons cognac
4 tablespoons grated Swiss
cheese

Toast the 4 slices of Pepperidge Farm bread until lightly
colored. Brush with clarified butter and leave in preheated oven
until crisp and golden.

Poach shrimps in simmering water with the sea salt and peppercorns for about 3 minutes. Cool in liquid, drain, and remove
shells and devein.

To prepare the sauce, combine the wine and tomato paste in
a small saucepan and reduce to ½ cup. Cook shallots, carrots,
and onions in 4 tablespoons butter and the oil, over moderate
heat, until lightly browned. Add the reduced wine, 1 cup water,
and herb bouquet, cover, and simmer about 20 minutes. Strain
sauce into another pan and reduce to about 1 cup. Stir in the 2

tablespoons flamed cognac, cream, and pieces of butter. Whisk in the cornstarch and water until it thickens.

Reheat the shrimps in 6 tablespoons butter and 2 tablespoons cognac for a minute. Drain, reserving juices, and place the shrimps on the toast. Stir the reserved pan juices into the sauce, coat the shrimps with sauce, sprinkle lightly with the cheese, and glaze quickly under broiler.

SERVES 4

TUNA FISH MARGUERY

(The famous recipe from the old Marguery Restaurant in New York)

1 (13-ounce) can white tuna, cut into pieces	2 tablespoons capers
	1 cup mayonnaise
3 fresh tomatoes, blanched, peeled, seeded, and cut in eighths	2 tablespoons ketchup
	2 tablespoons tarragon vinegar
3 hard-boiled eggs, cut in quarters lengthwise, then cut in half	Dash of cayenne pepper
	Salt and pepper to taste
	1 cup light cream

Mix all ingredients except the cream and then gently thin with the cream. Cook this mixture in a double boiler and, when hot, serve on pieces of crisp sautéed toast done in clarified butter. Decorate with watercress.

SERVES 4

SOLE IN SARAN THREE DIFFERENT WAYS

Watching my grandson, a chef in France, using this new method of cooking in Saran wrap inspired me to try my hand.

About 3 fillets of sole (or   Salt and pepper
    flounder)   Saran wrap

Cut fillet of sole into 8 pieces 3 inches by 4 inches and pound them between wax paper until paper-thin. Sprinkle with salt and pepper, fill each with about 2 tablespoons of one of the following fillings, and roll up. Tear off 8 pieces of Saran wrap about 10 inches long, butter the center of each one, place a rolled fillet in center of wrap, and roll tightly so it overlaps completely. Twist ends, one to the right, the other to the left, and tie a firm knot at each end of roll (I use a dish towel so I can have a firm, dry grip). When ready to cook, place all tied rolls in 2 to 3 inches simmering water for about 7 minutes, turning with a slotted spoon. When done, remove to paper towels with slotted spoon, cut off the knots on each end, and unwrap. Place on hot platter, pour sauce over, and decorate with Parsley en Pluches*.
SERVES 4

Filling Number I
Spinach

Cook 1¼ pounds fresh Spinach*, place in center of fish, and roll as directed (if necessary, you may use frozen leaf spinach). Serve sole with Hollandaise Sauce* and Parsley en Pluches*.

Filling Number II
Shrimp Mousse

½ pound raw shrimp, peeled and deveined
Salt and pepper to taste
½ cup heavy cream
Pinch of cayenne pepper
Pinch of grated nutmeg
1 egg

Place all ingredients in Cuisinart and process with knife blade to a fine purée for a filling. Proceed as directed and serve with Pink Fish Sauce (recipe follows).

Filling Number III
Salmon Mousse

Use ½ pound fresh salmon (or 2 slices 1½ inches thick), removing all bones and skin. Proceed as for Shrimp Mousse and serve sole with the same Pink Fish Sauce (recipe follows).

Hollandaise Sauce* is also good with all of these fillings.

3 shallots, chopped finely in Cuisinart	½ cup dry white wine
2 cups fish stock or clam juice	

Add the chopped shallots to the fish stock and wine and reduce to about 1¼ cups.

2 tablespoons butter	1 cup heavy cream
2½ tablespoons all-purpose flour	1 teaspoon imported tomato paste

Make a roux of the butter and flour, add the heavy cream, and reduce to about ⅔ cup. Strain fish stock through a very fine sieve and add to the reduced cream with tomato paste. This will make a lovely pale pink sauce. You may add cooked shrimps or lobster pieces to your sauce for an extra-special occasion, decorating with small oval-shaped puff pastries, cut out as directed under Puff Pastry*.

VARIEGATED MARINATED FISH

Marinate all day 12 large oysters, 12 chunks of any white fish (pompano, sole, bluefish, etc., with skin removed), 12 bay scallops, 12 pieces of lump crab meat, and 12 pieces of lobster (Maine preferred, but Florida lobster will do, though they are tougher). Different kinds of fish may be used.

Marinade

½ cup olive oil
Juice of 2 lemons
¼ cup tarragon vinegar

3 tablespoons fresh or 1½
   tablespoons dried tarragon
A little black pepper

Have butcher slice 1 pound bacon as thin as possible. Drain the marinade off the fish, wrap each piece in bacon, and slide onto skewers, alternating with a cherry tomato. (Alternate: Mushrooms may also be wrapped in bacon.) Cover your broiler with aluminum foil, making slits to fit openings in broiler pan. Preheat broiler and place skewers on pan and broil 3 minutes on each side until bacon is crisp.

Arrange Fluffy Rice* on a hot platter and put skewers on top. Decorate with sprigs of watercress or parsley between each skewer. Serve with Béarnaise Sauce* or Hollandaise Sauce*.
SERVES 6

Desserts

Desserts

APRICOT OR PRUNE SOUFFLÉ

6 egg whites, at room
   temperature
¼ cup granulated sugar

1¼ cups puréed apricots or
   prunes*

Beat egg whites to a soft peak, then gradually add sugar as you continue beating. Fold in the apricot purée. Turn mixture into the top of a 2½-quart double boiler (preferably a Revere) which has been buttered and sprinkled with sugar, including the lid, as soufflé will rise to the top and push up the lid as it cooks. Cover and cook over boiling water for 1 hour. Turn out onto a serving platter, garnish with a ring of whipped cream, and top with shaved almonds lightly browned in the oven.

The only trick to this soufflé is that the water must never boil away. The soufflé can be kept waiting for 40 minutes after it is cooked; if you do so, however, be sure to check and see that there is water in the bottom of the double boiler and turn heat down very low.

SERVES 6

* Dried apricots cooked with 1 cup sugar and water just to cover, then puréed. Be sure purée is thick and not runny. For prune purée, cook dried pitted prunes (which have been soaked in water) in water just to cover, with a squeeze of lemon, until soft. Purée in food processor, adding sugar to your taste (they need very little).

PRUNACOT SOUFFLÉ

This is a different way of serving apricots and prunes together. First prepare ½ recipe of each soufflé (see preceding recipe), placing the apricot mixture in the bottom of the double boiler and covering it with the prune mixture. Proceed as in preceding recipe. When you turn soufflé out, it is half prune and half apricot.

SERVES 6

SEVEN-LAYER CAKE

Slice a 10¾-ounce Sara Lee pound cake lengthwise in 7 thin slices while still cold but not frozen. Make frosting as follows:

Place 1⅓ bags of Nestlé semisweet chocolate Toll House morsels (or 8 ounces) in blender or Cuisinart, add ¼ cup boiling water, cover, and blend. Remove cover and add 4 egg yolks and 2 teaspoons of vanilla. Blend with cover off and then add ¼ pound very soft butter in 4 parts. Blend until smooth. Spread between layers and on top and sides of cake. Use cake comb or tines of a fork to make a design on top. You can also use this frosting—adding the grated rind of 2 oranges—between lady fingers or slices of angel food cake. Serve with fruit.

If you wish a mocha flavor, add 1 teaspoon of powdered coffee to the hot water.

NOTE: The pound cake makes very good cookies by slicing thin, cutting in half, and baking in 350° F. oven until dry.

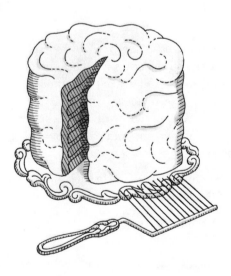

BROWN SUGAR CRUST

This is something that I worked out, first trying it on crème brûlée. As you probably know, it is difficult to sprinkle brown sugar on top of the custard and then run it under the broiler. Sometimes the sugar will sink into the custard instead of staying on top. So here is a quick, easy method and several different ways of serving it.

Butter a cookie sheet well. With your fingertips, pat medium brown sugar on this sheet to make a thin, lacy layer. You should be able to see the tin in some spots through the sugar. Make a paper pattern of the top of the dish that you are going to use and lay this pattern on the brown sugar. Remove the extra sugar surrounding the pattern with a spatula and discard paper pattern. Put cookie sheet under broiler flame until sugar is slightly burned and glazed, watching it every second. Take the sheet out and, when it is slightly cool, start loosening the edges of the sugar with a spatula. Finally the crust will come away from the sheet looking like a large praline. Place crust over the rim of the dish.

Brown sugar crusts may be frozen.

Ways of serving:

1. Fill the center of a serving bowl with vanilla ice cream and surround with fresh strawberries, peaches, or other fruit, sprinkled with a little sugar and soaked in brandy or a favorite liqueur. Then place Brown Sugar Crust, made to fit the rim of the bowl, on top. When the crust is cracked, the inside is a surprise, and the ice cream and fruit are delicious with the crunchy sugar pieces.

2. Try Brown Sugar Crust on a rich floating island, rather than crème brûlée, and serve with fruits. It is not as rich.

3. Make a tart applesauce, place Brown Sugar Crust over rim of dish, and serve with sour cream.

4. Cook blueberries, fresh or frozen, with sugar and a little water until thickened, season with lemon juice, and thicken the

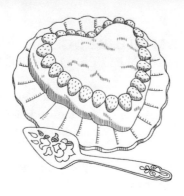

blueberries with a little potato starch mixed with cold water. Pour into serving dish and, when cool, top with Brown Sugar Crust.

5. Remove seedless grapes from stem and wipe (do not wash). Stir in sour cream until each grape is coated. Pack in a flat dish with sides. Chill for 4 hours. Place Brown Sugar Crust on top and serve with curaçao or crème de cacao.

6. Brown Sugar Candy Bowl: Proceed as for Brown Sugar Crust. Watch and when melted all over (not burned), remove. Using spatula, shape it back into original size of round. As it cools, try running spatula underneath. When it is free from pan, remove. Wearing cotton gloves, quickly put it on a buttered mold turned upside down. (Use a soufflé dish for a large bowl or individual soufflé dish for a small bowl.) Shape at once by pleating sides around mold with fingers. Remove, place at once in a tightly covered tin, and place in freezer. To serve, fill with ice cream, custard, fruit, floating islands, or whatever you wish. With a serving spoon, crack the candy bowl, serving pieces of it with the filling. (Be sure your dish is ice cold.) Candy bowls will remain for a long time in freezer. Keep any broken bits of sugar to sprinkle on oranges as a dessert, or on ice cream. If you have trouble with your first candy bowl, crack it up, keep the bits for dessert topping, and try again.

EMMIE BERG'S
CHOCOLATE POTS DE CRÈME

½ cup heavy cream
½ cup granulated sugar
3 tablespoons Droste cocoa

4 egg yolks, lightly beaten
Grated rind of 2 oranges or 1
    tablespoon brandy

In a saucepan, combine cream, sugar, and cocoa and bring to a boil. Remove pan from fire and stir in egg yolks. Return to low heat and cook, stirring constantly with a wooden spoon, until thickened. Stir in grated orange peel or brandy. Pour the cream into pots de crème cups and place in the refrigerator until thoroughly chilled.

Since this cream does not have to be baked in the oven, it is an excellent recipe to use for those beautiful old china pots de crème.

SERVES 4

CHOCOLATE SOUFFLÉ (BAVEUSE)

6 squares unsweetened
  chocolate
¾ cup granulated sugar
3 tablespoons butter
3 tablespoons all-purpose
  flour

1½ cups milk
8 egg whites and 6 yolks
3 tablespoons vanilla
2 tablespoons superfine sugar
  (on top)

Put the 6 whole squares of unsweetened chocolate in the top of a double boiler. Add the granulated sugar and 2 tablespoons hot water from the tap. Melt over simmering water, stirring occasionally.

In a pan, melt the butter and stir in the flour. When the roux is smooth, gradually add the milk. Cook and stir over medium heat until thick and smooth and add the melted chocolate. Beat the egg yolks with a rotary beater until light in color and combine with the warm cream sauce. Cool, and add the vanilla. Beat the egg whites until very stiff. Stir quickly into the soufflé mixture one quarter of the egg whites, then fold in remaining whites carefully with an up-and-down movement. Pour into an unbuttered shallow baking dish (this is necessary because of the quick cooking). Sprinkle with the superfine sugar and bake in preheated 385° F. oven for 12 to 14 minutes.* Serve with whipped cream, flavored with grated orange rind to taste and 1 tablespoon vanilla, or with vanilla ice cream.

Cook 18 minutes for a firmer soufflé.

SERVES 6

* This soufflé can be baked while you are eating the main course.

COEUR À LA CRÈME

2 (8-ounce) packages cream
cheese

1 cup heavy cream, whipped
½ cup sour cream

Keep cream cheese at room temperature until soft. Blend cheese with the whipped cream, then mix in the sour cream. Be sure that there are no lumps. Line a heart-shaped mold with damp cheesecloth and fill with the cheese mixture. Place the mold in the refrigerator for several hours before serving. Remove cheese from mold to dessert plate by turning mold upside down. Remove cheesecloth and outline the heart of cheese with strawberries.

Individual heart molds may also be used.

SERVES 6

COFFEE COEUR À LA CRÈME

Follow the preceding recipe for Coeur à la Crème. Before molding, stir in 3 tablespoons confectioners' sugar and 2 teaspoons powdered coffee dissolved in 2 scant tablespoons boiling water and cooled.

This is wonderful with strawberries, but also very interesting surrounded by seedless grapes soaked in a little brandy and drained well.

SERVES 6

Have you ever tried Jim Beard's strawberries marinated in Armagnac, sugar, and black pepper? A marvelous flavor!

MARY APPLEQUIST'S CORNFLAKE COOKIES

½ cup butter
1 cup granulated sugar
2 eggs, lightly beaten
4 cups cornflakes

½ cup chopped pecans
(optional)
1 teaspoon vanilla

Preheat oven to 375° F. (moderate). Cream the butter and sugar. Stir in the eggs, cornflakes, nuts, and vanilla. Drop batter by tablespoons on a buttered Teflon cookie sheet and bake for about 6 minutes, or until browned.

These cookies can be molded by placing, while still hot, in a cupcake pan and patting down with your fingers to make a cup. The cups can be filled with any ice cream or sorbet.

MAKES 32 COOKIES

An amusing episode happened last summer while I was in Simone Beck's house in France. I was not too familiar with the oven and did not have a Teflon cookie sheet. The cookies came out a complete flop and stuck. In anger, I scraped them off so they were in chunky pieces. An idea popped into my head, and for dessert that night we had balls of vanilla ice cream rolled in the cookie bits, with a butterscotch sauce. Superb!

CREAM PUFFS AND PROFITEROLES

Prepare dough as for Gnocchi with Mornay Sauce*, adding 1 tablespoon of sugar to the mixture and omitting the cheese. Preheat oven to 425° F. Spoon dough the size you wish onto a cookie sheet and bake 15 to 20 minutes, depending on the size. One rounded tablespoon makes a small puff; 2 rounded tablespoons, a large puff; 1 rounded teaspoon, a profiterole. Reduce heat to 300° F. and bake 5 minutes longer. Prick sides to release steam and cool.

Profiteroles are tiny cream puffs filled with whipped cream or ice cream with a hot chocolate sauce poured over them, a wonderful dessert.

You can make cream puff swans, with small end of pastry tube, by piping the head and neck onto a cookie sheet. Watch carefully, as they bake quickly! When baked, you can dip the beak in melted chocolate and make a chocolate eye. Slice off top of cream puff, cut in half, and stick the halves in the whipped cream or ice cream filling to resemble wings.

Cream puffs freeze beautifully, either filled or unfilled.

MAKES 6 TO 8 CREAM PUFFS OR ABOUT 24 PROFITEROLES

I had an amusing swan in Italy, filled with hot creamed chicken with wings of large potato chips and the neck and head made of the dough.

CRÊPES

4 eggs
4 teaspoons sugar
½ teaspoon salt
1 cup all-purpose flour

½ cup milk and ½ cup
water combined
2 tablespoons stale beer

Beat the eggs, sugar, and salt lightly until the whites and yolks are blended. Add the flour and milk alternately, beating constantly with a rotary or electric beater. Add beer, and let batter stand at room temperature for 1 hour or more.

Butter an 8-inch crêpe pan lightly, preferably with clarified butter. When butter bubbles and pan is hot, add ¼ cup batter and quickly turn and tip the pan to spread the batter as thin as paper. Brown, turn with a spatula, and brown the other side. Roll, or fold twice to form a triangle. Keep in a warm place, but not in the oven, for that would dry the crêpes. Serve hot.
SERVES 6

If you wish to use the crêpes for a first course, use only 1 teaspoon sugar in the batter. Fill crêpe with creamed mushrooms or crab meat. Remember to flavor creamed mushrooms with dry vermouth.

Fines Herbes Crêpes

2 teaspoons fresh tarragon
2 teaspoons chives

2 shallots (or 1 onion)
2 teaspoons parsley

All the above finely chopped and added to the crêpe batter give a wonderful flavor. If you do not have fresh herbs, use Spice Islands fines herbes.

CRÊPE SOUFFLÉ APRICOT

Prepare crêpes for dessert according to the Crêpes* recipe and fold twice into quarters. Lifting top layer, fill with about 3 heaping tablespoons Apricot Soufflé* mixture and arrange in buttered shallow baking dish. (Be sure some of the filling is exposed so it can rise.) Bake in preheated 425° F. oven for about 5 minutes, until filling rises and browns lightly. Flame with hot brandy, or any liqueur, and sprinkle with sliced, toasted almonds.

I do a Cheese Soufflé* the same way by reducing the sugar to 2 teaspoons and deleting the flaming with brandy and the almonds. Fill the crêpe with the cheese soufflé mixture and fold over once. Bake as above and serve on top of a Mornay Sauce*.

CRÈME BRÛLÉE À L'ORANGE

In the top of a double boiler, scald 3 cups of heavy cream. Beat 6 egg yolks in a bowl and *gradually* beat in 6 tablespoons sugar. Beat the mixture until it is light and creamy. Slowly add the warm cream to the egg yolks and add 2 tablespoons orange-flavored liqueur and 1 tablespoon grated orange rind.

Return the mixture to the double boiler over hot but *not boiling* water and cook it, stirring constantly with a wooden spoon until it thickens and coats a silver spoon. Pour the custard into a shallow glass baking dish and chill thoroughly. Top with pre-made Brown Sugar Crust*. If you wish a regular crème brûlée, follow the above recipe, adding 1 full tablespoon vanilla and omitting the orange liqueur and orange rind.

SERVES 6

NOTE: A quick way is simply to flavor sour cream with vanilla and place in shallow casserole with Brown Sugar Crust* on top.

FRUITS AND MANY WAYS TO SERVE THEM

1. Slice peeled ripe Bartlett pears into a bowl and serve with an orange sauce made as follows: in a saucepan, mix 2 teaspoons potato starch with 3 tablespoons orange juice. Stir in 1 cup orange juice and bring to a boil. Remove from the stove and stir in another cup of orange juice. Pour the sauce over the pears, which have just been peeled and sprinkled with lemon juice, and serve ice-cold. This will keep several days in the refrigerator.

2. Poach a peeled, cored pear very lightly in a sugar syrup. Drain and dry with paper towel. When cold, coat with soft cream cheese mixed with sour cream. Stud with seedless grapes and surround with cold raspberry or strawberry sauce.

3. Core and peel a raw pear and cut in half. Lemon juice on pears will keep them white. Arrange green leaves (a Galax leaf, which you can buy at your florist, or fresh leaves from your gar-

den) on a round platter. Place a bowl in the center, filled with ice-cold thickened orange sauce (see Number 1, above) or the sauce for Mandarin Oranges Au Bon Goût*. Surround with the pear halves filled with balls of lemon or orange sorbet, and sprinkle grated orange rind on top.

4. Vanilla ice cream, grated orange peel, and curaçao.

5. Ice-cold canned Kadota figs, drained. Top with sour cream and pass crème de cacao.

6. Vanilla ice cream with lemon juice. The juice may be thickened in the same way as the orange juice in Number 1, above.

7. Yogurt surrounded with any combination of fresh fruits.

8. The Duchess of Windsor told me that her favorite dessert was lemon sorbet mounded in the center of a platter and surrounded by sour cream and sliced fresh figs. (Kiwi fruit may be substituted for figs.)

9. Coat seedless grapes with sour cream, refrigerate 2 hours, then mold with your hands to look like a large bunch of grapes, having saved the stem to put at one end with green leaves that you have on hand to resemble grape leaves. Serve with brown sugar.

NOTE: The Waring Blender Ice Cream Parlor machine is a must in my kitchen for sorbet or ice cream.

MANDARIN ORANGES AU BON GOÛT

Put 1 envelope Knox unflavored gelatin in 1 cup orange juice. Dissolve over low heat and cool. Open a can of mandarin oranges and drain off juice. Place 9 sections in a row on paper towels. These make 1 small orange. Assemble sections loosely in hand, which you hold over a bowl. Pour a little orange gelatin over sections, seeing that gelatin coats each slice. Place in 2-inch muffin pan. Add more orange gelatin over top. Refrigerate 2 hours. (Muffin pan has room for 12 oranges.) To remove from pan, run sharp knife around edge and remove orange with teaspoon. Garnish with sprig of mint on top. Serve 2 oranges per person, with following sauce.

I make this dessert the day before I wish to serve it.

1 CAN MAKES 4 ORANGES

Fruit Sauce

In a saucepan, put 1 (10-ounce) jar currant jelly, ⅔ cup orange juice, the juice of 1 lemon, and ¼ teaspoon cinnamon. Place pan over a low flame and heat until the jelly melts. Meanwhile select 4 large oranges that can be peeled easily and, with a vegetable peeler, pare off orange portion of the rind in paper-thin slices. Cut these into julienne strips and add them to the melted jelly. Increase heat until syrup boils and simmer, uncovered, for 15 minutes.

When cool, stir in curaçao or any favorite liqueur, to taste, and a little brandy. Chill.

This sauce is delicious over any fruit.

MANDARIN ORANGES MYRTLE

Make a cup of any sherbet or ice by placing sherbet in a 3-inch muffin tin with an indentation the size of an orange. Cover with foil and freeze. Place orange in molded sherbet cup with a green Galax leaf (or any large green leaf) underneath and garnish with a sprig of mint. Serve on an ice-cold platter, allowing 1 per person.

Another way is to mound mandarin oranges in a pyramid and stick broken bits of Brown Sugar Candy Bowl* all over. Surround with green leaves.

FROZEN LIMES OR LEMONS

For each serving, cut a slice from the top of a large lemon or lime and set aside. Clean out the inside, using a sharp knife and then a spoon or potato baller. Fill fruit shells with lime or lemon sherbet, ice, or ice cream. Wrap in foil, stand in egg containers, and freeze. Take out of freezer a few minutes before serving. Push a hole in center of ice and, just before serving, fill hole with apricot or any liqueur. Make a hole with an ice pick in the top slice, place a green leaf or mint leaf in the hole, and serve. Use a teaspoon instead of a dessert spoon for service. These shells may be washed, refilled, frozen, and will always be ready for any unexpected guest.

The bottom of either fruit must be sliced off so that the fruit will sit flat when served.

LIME POTS DE CRÈME AND TOPPING

½ cup lime juice (from Key
  limes if possible)
1 (14-ounce) can sweetened
  condensed milk, plus ¼
  cup fresh milk

2 egg whites
2 egg yolks
1 tablespoon grated lime rind
1 drop only green food
  coloring

Squeeze limes and open can of milk. Beat egg whites in a
small bowl. Beat egg yolks in a large bowl, add the condensed
and fresh milk, then gradually add the grated lime rind, juice,
and green food coloring. Fold in the egg whites. Chill in pot de
crème cups.

For the topping: Place 12 graham crackers and 5 ginger
snaps together with ½ cup confectioners' sugar in Cuisinart.
Pour the blended mixture into a bowl and stir in 4 tablespoons
melted butter. Butter a cookie sheet without sides and roll the
cracker mixture with a rolling pin into a crust that is about 5 by
6 inches. Do not let it get too thin. Bake for 10 to 12 minutes in
350° F. oven, watching it carefully after the first 5 minutes.
Crush into coarse powder with a rolling pin and sprinkle on top
of lime pots de crème. Place a spoonful of whipped cream in the
center of each.

This topping may be served on many dessert dishes, such as
apples, blueberries, peaches, or even cooked fresh strawberries. It
will keep in a tightly covered jar, in the refrigerator, for a very
long time.

SERVES 6

CUISINART PIECRUST

I use this piecrust for many things. Yields one 8- , 9- , or 10-inch pastry shell.

1½ cups Wondra
quick-mixing flour
¼ cup (½ stick) chilled
unsalted butter, cut into
1-inch cubes
¼ cup chilled solid vegetable
shortening

¼ teaspoon salt
¼ cup cold water (or just
enough to form ball of
dough)

In Cuisinart, blend the instant flour, butter, shortening, and salt until mixture is crumbly and pieces are the size of small peas.

Add the water and mix until the dough comes clean from bowl and forms a ball. Flatten dough into an 8-inch circle, enclose in plastic wrap, and place in refrigerator for 30 minutes.

Preheat oven to 400° F. Place dough on a lightly floured surface. Roll out dough, cut to desired size, and bake.

I often cut chicken, bird, or fish pastries with cookie molds to decorate a dish. Easier, crisp, and not too much pastry! The chicken shape illustrated is the actual size for a piecrust pattern to decorate a shallow dish of creamed chicken, for example.

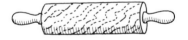

SINFUL LEMON TARTS

Using Cuisinart Piecrust* recipe, make bite-size tarts on back of tin molds and prick with a fork. Bake in hot oven until light brown. Fill with Lemon Cream (recipe follows) just before serving, adding a dot of whipped cream on top (optional).
SERVES 8

Lemon Cream

½ cup sugar   ¼ cup sweet butter
Juice and grated rind of 2   5 egg yolks
   lemons

Combine sugar, lemon juice, rind, and sweet butter in a heavy saucepan. Allow them to melt over low heat. In another pan, beat egg yolks until light and fluffy and, over low heat, add butter mixture slowly, beating all the time and removing from heat if steam appears, until it becomes thick.

This lemon cream may be used for cake filling and for tarts, both tiny and large, and keeps for over a week in the refrigerator.

An attractive way to serve these is to alternate tarts, some with one strawberry placed on a small amount of lemon cream, and the others filled with the lemon cream.

COLD ORANGE SOUFFLÉ

1 cup cold water
2 envelopes Knox unflavored
  gelatin
8 eggs, separated
½ teaspoon salt

2 (6-ounce) cans frozen
  orange concentrate
1 cup sugar
1 cup heavy cream
Grated rind of 1 large orange

Place water in top of a double boiler and sprinkle the gelatin over the surface to soften. Beat the egg yolks lightly and add salt. Combine egg yolks and gelatin mixture and beat well. Place over boiling water and cook, stirring constantly, until gelatin dissolves and mixture thickens a bit—about 4 minutes. Remove from double boiler and add orange concentrate. Chill over ice until mixture drops from a spoon into soft mounds. Beat the egg whites a little, then gradually beat in the sugar and continue beating until the egg whites are stiff. Whip the cream. Fold the whites into the orange mixture, add the grated rind, and then fold in the cream.

Arrange a collar of double wax paper, which has been buttered on the side facing the soufflé, around a 1½-quart soufflé dish. The collar should come 2 inches above the top of the dish. Fasten with string and paper clip. Pour mixture into dish and chill until firm. Remove collar and press Pralin Powder*, macaroon crumbs, or powdered toasted almonds around the exposed sides of the soufflé. Decorate top with orange or mandarin sections (optional) and whipped cream forced through a pastry tube.

SERVES 10 TO 12

This soufflé may also be served individually in hollowed-out orange cups. Place a buttered wax-paper collar around orange cup. Collar should be 1 inch above rim of orange. Fill, chill, and garnish with whipped cream.

Concentrated lime can be used in place of orange and the soufflé served in hollowed-out lime cups. This mixture can also be made with grape concentrate, eliminating the sugar.

MERINGUE SHELLS

Beat 4 egg whites with an electric mixer until foamy. Add ½ teaspoon cream of tartar and ¼ teaspoon salt and beat until a soft peak forms, then beat in 1¼ cups sugar, 1 tablespoon at a time. Continue beating until sugar is dissolved and the mixture is stiff and glossy, 8 to 10 minutes. Mix in 1 teaspoon each lemon juice and vanilla. Cover 2 cookie sheets with brown paper or cooking parchment. Use a spatula to shape two 9-inch shells (or eight 3½-inch shells). Place in a very hot oven (475° F. for large shells, 450° F. for small shells). Close door, turn off heat, and leave overnight, or for 4 hours minimum. This is especially good for a humid climate.

PEAR AND CHEESE

Peel and core pear, leaving stem on top. Squeeze lemon juice over pear (if done ahead of time). Cut top one-third of the way down and save. Stuff with any soft cheese, such as Brie or Camembert. Cover with stemmed top. Serve on a green leaf. A delicious dessert accompanied by white wine.

PINEAPPLE BIRD

Cut pineapple lengthwise, leaving all green leaves on bottom portion, then hollow out pineapple. Fill center with a macédoine (cut-up fresh fruits that have been soaked in kirsch or any liqueur). Place lemon, lime, or pineapple ice on top of this. Cut lengthwise the slice of pineapple that you took off top, inserting these pieces like the wings of a swan. To make neck, use crookneck squash, slicing bottom to hug the pineapple. Secure with toothpicks. Place 2 cloves as eyes.

SERVES 6

PUMPKIN POT DE CRÈME

(A light dessert after Thanksgiving dinner)

½ cup Del Monte pumpkin (strain through sieve to remove liquid)
½ cup half-and-half
⅓ cup brown sugar
3 beaten egg yolks
1 scant teaspoon cinnamon
½ teaspoon powdered ginger (scant)
Pinch of salt
¼ teaspoon powdered cloves
¼ teaspoon powdered nutmeg
1 teaspoon brandy (optional)
½ teaspoon vanilla
Grated rind of 1 orange

Place pumpkin, half-and-half, and sugar in a saucepan and heat, then slowly add beaten egg yolks and beat with wire whip until quite thick. Add all of the spices, brandy, vanilla, and grated orange. Place in 5 pots de crème and, when cool, refrigerate.

SERVES 4 OR 5

Here are three ways of serving:

1. Place a teaspoon of whipped cream on top.

2. Put crumbled cookie crust topping from Lime Pots de Crème and Topping* on top, with or without cream.

3. Place in half an orange shell and top with either of the above.

RASPBERRY DESSERT OR SAUCE

2 boxes frozen raspberries
¼ cup granulated sugar

Juice of ½ lemon
2 tablespoons potato starch

Cook raspberries with the sugar and lemon juice until soft. Mash through a sieve and add the potato starch mixed with ½ cup cold water. Bring to a boil, stirring; and, when clear and thickened, pour into a baking dish. Serve hot, flambéed with rum, or serve icy-cold. To flambé, pour heated rum over the surface and set rum aflame.

If a thinner sauce is desired, use less potato starch.

SERVES 4 TO 6

This sauce is delicious poured over a whole peeled peach or a fresh or baked pear studded with toasted shaved almonds.

SOUFFLÉ SAUCE

Beat 2 egg yolks. Gradually beat in about 1 cup confectioners' sugar, or more, until mixture is too stiff to beat. In another bowl, whip 1 cup cream, cover, and put in refrigerator. Just before serving, combine egg mixture with whipped cream and flavor with grand marnier or brandy to taste. This is good on all fruit desserts and with soufflés.

SERVES 6.

TODAY'S GRANDMOTHER'S RICH MAN–POOR MAN RICE PUDDING

This is an old family recipe that was made once a week on "laundry day." It was cooked for about 4 hours in the oven of a coal stove so it could be stirred while one was doing the ironing. Whole milk was used, so everything has changed—the milk, the stove, and the labor!

5 tablespoons long-grain rice
4 tablespoons granulated
  sugar
1 quart skimmed milk

1 pint heavy cream
Pinch of salt
2½ tablespoons vanilla

Grease a baking dish and put in all ingredients except vanilla. Preheat oven to 350° F. and bake for 1½ hours, stirring at least 6 or 7 times, each time after a skin has formed on top and become slightly browned. This is what gives the pudding its flavor, and the skim milk makes it possible and does not curdle.

When pudding is thick, remove from oven, add the vanilla, and run under broiler to give it the final brown top.

If you wish to prepare individual servings, spoon rice pudding into ramekins and place them on a cookie sheet before running under broiler.

Serve cold.

SERVES 6

HERRICK'S UNUSUAL SOUFFLÉ

½ cup Cream of Wheat
3 cups milk
1 teaspoon salt, plus a pinch
¼ cup sugar
1 tablespoon butter

3 eggs, separated
1 teaspoon vanilla
½ cup light brown sugar
½ cup slivered almonds,
  toasted

Cook the Cream of Wheat, milk, 1 teaspoon salt, and sugar in double boiler until thick. Add the butter, well-beaten egg yolks, and vanilla. Cool. Beat egg whites with a pinch of salt until they stand in peaks. Fold whites into cooled mixture and place in shallow Pyrex dish. Preheat oven to 350° F. (moderate) and bake for ½ hour. Sprinkle thickly with the brown sugar and brown under broiler. Serve hot with toasted shaved almonds on top, accompanied with whipped cream and thick raspberry or strawberry sauce.

SERVES 6

STRAWBERRY CINNAMON TOASTS

(A quick and light dessert)

Sauté large rounds of dried Pepperidge Farm thin-sliced white bread, in clarified butter, on both sides. While still slightly warm, place them in a mixture of cinnamon and sugar to taste, which you have ready on a piece of wax paper. (This may be done ahead of time.)

When you are ready to serve, slice large, fresh strawberries (slice down from top of stem, not using the outsides or curved edges). Cover the cinnamon rounds with strawberry slices.

Decorate with whipped cream, sour cream, or Cool Whip, using a pastry bag.

These can also be made with small toast rounds and 1 whole strawberry, pierced with a toothpick through the strawberry and toast. Serve 4 to a person, or fewer if berries are very large.

COLD STRAWBERRY SOUFFLÉ

Tie a 30-by-6-inch band of buttered wax paper around outside rim of a 7½-by-2¾-inch (1- to 1½-quart) porcelain soufflé dish so that it stands 3 inches above the rim. Make 3½ cups of strawberry purée by blending 3 pints hulled fresh strawberries in blender at high speed. Strain through a sieve.

In a saucepan, combine ½ cup granulated sugar, 3 envelopes unflavored gelatin, and 1¾ cups of the strawberry purée. Stir over medium heat until gelatin is completely dissolved. Let cool. Add 2 tablespoons lemon or orange juice and the remaining purée. Chill over ice in a bowl, stirring constantly, until the mixture is like unbeaten egg white.

In a large electric mixer bowl, at high speed, beat 8 egg whites with ¼ teaspoon salt until light and foamy. Gradually add ½ cup granulated sugar, beating until egg whites hold soft peaks. Whip 2 cups heavy cream, until cream holds its shape, and pour over egg whites. Now add the chilled purée and the grated rind of 2 oranges. With a rubber spatula, carefully fold in all ingredients. Pour into soufflé dish and refrigerate 2 hours, or until set. Carefully remove wax-paper band. Decorate edge that stands above dish with Pralin Powder* and place some large strawberries with stems on top. Serve with whipped cream, to which you have added 1 tablespoon curaçao and more grated orange rind, plus sliced fresh strawberries (or frozen ones and unsweetened whipped cream).
SERVES 10 TO 12

NOTE: The soufflé may be made with frozen strawberries, too. Substitute 2 (1-pound) packages frozen whole strawberries in heavy syrup, thawed, for the fresh ones. Reduce the sugar, blended with the gelatin, to ¼ cup. Follow other directions exactly.

DEEP-DISH STRAWBERRY PIE

Make a paper pattern of the top of the baking dish. Using Cuisinart Piecrust* recipe, make pastry the size of the pattern, bake, and place on the top at the last minute. This ensures that the crust is always crisp at serving time.

Prepare strawberries as follows:

4 boxes fresh strawberries
1½ cups water
¼ cup sugar (about)

3 tablespoons potato starch
Red food coloring (optional)
Grated rind of 1 large orange

Cook 1 box of washed and hulled berries in 1½ cups water and ¼ cup sugar (or to taste). When berries are soft and mushy, strain and pour hot sauce into pan. Add the 3 tablespoons potato starch, diluted in 4 tablespoons cold water. Heat and stir until thick. Remove from stove. Pour into baking dish and add the rest of hulled berries, a few drops of red coloring, and the grated orange rind. When cool, refrigerate. Serve with pastry crust on top and whipped cream or ice cream. This may also be served at room temperature.

SERVES 6

COLD ZABAGLIONE QUO VADIS

In the top of a double boiler, combine 4 egg yolks and ¾ cup each of sugar and dry white wine or Marsala. Cook the mixture over simmering water for about 10 minutes, beating continuously with a sauce whisk or a rotary beater, until it is so thick that it will float a spoon. Set pan into a bowl of cracked ice and continue to beat the Zabaglione until it is very cold. Pour into sherbet glasses and chill it well.
SERVES 3 TO 4

I often serve cold Zabaglione in a hollowed-out orange cup, adding grated orange rind.

QUICK ZABAGLIONE SAUCE

4 egg yolks   ½ cup sugar
¾ cup white wine

Beat egg yolks in pan with wire whip; add wine and sugar. Place over medium heat and beat constantly, raising pan when a little steam appears. Continue beating and return to heat. Repeat until sauce thickens. For dessert, add 2 extra egg yolks and ¼ cup Marsala instead of white wine.
SERVES 4

SWAN LAKE

Light brown sugar
2½ cups scalded milk
6 egg yolks
⅓ cup sugar
2 tablespoons vanilla

Pinch of salt
6 egg whites
½ cup superfine sugar (or
  more)

Difficult but spectacular!

Make a cardboard pattern of a swan's head and neck about 2 inches high and, for the wings, make rounds about 2½ inches across with uneven edges on outside of wings. (The illustration is the actual size for the swan patterns.) On a well-buttered cookie sheet, sprinkle light brown sugar as thinly as in Brown Sugar Crust* about the size of each pattern. Place patterns on top of sugar and push away any extra sugar around them. Remove patterns and, high up under broiler, melt for a few seconds. Watch! Take out and use spatula, working quickly to re-form shape as it cools (this has to be freehand shaping) and then pushing spatula under sugar to loosen. When cool, these will be thin hard candies resembling the head and neck and wings of a swan. Place in a covered receptacle at once. These may be done days ahead and frozen.

Make custard sauce as follows: Pour the scalded milk over the egg yolks, slightly beaten with the ⅓ cup sugar. Stir in a double boiler with a wooden spoon until sauce coats a silver spoon. Add the vanilla and pinch of salt. Pour into a long flat oval dish with a little depth. Place in refrigerator until thickened and cold. I do this the night before.

Two hours before serving, beat the egg whites with ½ cup or more superfine sugar so they will stand up well. Place mounds of egg whites (about 3 heaping tablespoons) in *simmering* water (I use a long pan over two burners so I will have sufficient

room). Try to shape mounds higher on one end, turning each over once. Simmer for 3 to 4 minutes. To serve 6, make 2 large mounds and some smaller ones—Mama, Papa, and babies! Remove from water and place on rack to dry. When time comes to serve, place on the custard and quickly insert heads and wings.

Fresh strawberries, raspberries, or peaches are good with this.

SERVES 6

PRALIN POWDER

2½ cups nuts of your choice   ¼ cup water
     without skins   1 tablespoon vanilla
2 cups granulated sugar

Toast the nuts for about 10 to 15 minutes in 350° F. oven, stirring once in a while. Cook the sugar, water, and vanilla in a cast-iron pan over good heat until a caramel color, watching carefully. Add toasted nuts and stir until completely coated. Pour onto well-buttered baking sheet or marble. When cool and brittle, crack into pieces and pulverize in Cuisinart with knife blade. Will freeze in tightly covered jar for a very long time. Serve on cold soufflés and many other cold desserts.

Index

211